A Young Virginia Boatman Navigates the Civil War

Published for the Library at the Mariners' Museum by the
University of Virginia Press | Charlottesville and London
in association with the Port Hampton History Foundation

OTHER JOINT PUBLICATIONS

A briefe and true report of the new found land of Virginia
by Thomas Hariot (The 1590 Theodor de Bry Latin Edition)

A Young Virginia Boatman Navigates the Civil War

The Journals of George Randolph Wood

Compiled and Edited by Will Molineux

With Research Assistance from Theresa Hammond

Introductory Essay by Scott Nelson

University of Virginia Press

Printed in the United States of America on acid-free paper

First published 2010

9 8 7 6 5 4 3 2 1

LIBRARY OF CONGRESS CATALOGING-IN-PUBLICATION DATA

Wood, George Randolph, 1847–1920.
A young Virginia boatman navigates the Civil War : the journals of George Randolph Wood / compiled and edited by Will Molineux with research assistance from Theresa Hammond ; introductory essay by Scott Nelson.
p. cm.
Includes bibliographical references and index.
ISBN 978-0-8139-2903-3 (cloth : alk. paper)
1. Wood, George Randolph, 1847–1920—Diaries. 2. Boatmen—Virginia—Biography. 3. United States—History—Civil War, 1861–1865—Riverine operations—Sources. 4. Virginia—History—Civil War, 1861–1865—Riverine operations—Sources. 5. United States—History—Civil War, 1861–1865—Transportation—Sources. 6. Virginia—History—Civil War, 1861–1865—Transportation—Sources. 7. James River (Va.)—History, Military—19th century—Sources. 8. United States—History—Civil War, 1861–1865—Personal narratives, Confederate. I. Molineux, Will. II. Hammond, Theresa. III. Title.
E596.W66 2010
973.7′82—dc22

2009042707

For Dorothy Rouse-Bottom, a devoted advocate of historic Hampton

Contents

Maps and Illustrations

Maps

Illustrations

Representative pages from George Wood's journal appear on pp. 2, 28, 78, and 118

Navigating Allegiances in America's Civil War

George Randolph Wood's Brackish Odyssey

Scott Nelson, Legum Professor of History,
College of William and Mary

George Randolph Wood, like his father and his grandfather before him, worked on the James River, and from the river he would watch the Civil War unfold. A river pilot must have an encyclopedic memory of sandbars, rocks, and landing places. Young George's knowledge of the twists and bends of the river, its sharp currents and dangerous places, made him invaluable when the war started. The sharp eye for detail that is evident in this memoir—catfish in canals, slick Union overcoats, a merchant's name on a molasses barrel, soldiers asleep in wheat fields, the knee-high britches of a poor white teenager—makes Wood's memories of the Civil War vibrant and indelible. Wood navigated the water, the border between battlefield and home front, the line between Southern Unionist and Confederate, and the shifting boundary between slavery and freedom. Because his father was "a Union man," George and his brother Robert B. would take different sides during the conflict. George, with his photographic recall of scenes and settings, seems to have captured it all.[1]

1. I have been most influenced by Marcus Rediker's provocative call to study oceans, rivers, and waterways—the liminal spaces between nations—in his talk entitled "The Making of the Atlantic Working Classes," given at the biennial meeting of the Southern Labor Studies Conference in Miami in 2002. On the necessity of a young pilot's learning all the "islands, towns,

In his account of evacuating City Point, George shows off his claim to fame, his knowledge of every major landing on the James River. He describes how the Confederate sympathizers in his family evacuated Hampton in 1861, halting briefly upriver between Williamsburg and City Point (now Hopewell), and cannot resist describing the landings on the river, or showing that he knew the depth of each of its sandbars. He describes the prewar trade network that was destined to fade away: Virginia's flour, timber, and tobacco traded for South American coffee and guano. He tells us about the new Confederate trade network that will soon be a crucial part of the railroad corridor between Petersburg and points further South, and the tugs, schooners, steamboats, and barges that will ply the waters between City Point and Richmond. He also briefly describes the informal economy of slaves that "amused" his friends—the semi-licit barter between slaves and a Jewish grocer who took their homegrown eggs and chickens in exchange for imported coffee, linens, and sugar.

From his perspective on the water, Wood provides a fascinating discussion of crucial events in the American Civil War. Nearly every U.S. history textbook describes the three-way confrontation at Fort Monroe on May 24, 1861, between slaves, slaveholders, and the Union army with respect to the status of escapees. General Benjamin Butler's clever legal stratagem—designating escaped slaves as contraband of war—rendered them neither free men nor chattel but "captured" war goods, and thus allowed the Union army to use them as laborers. Yet few histories have described the Confederate army's ruthless response to the prospect of freed people's occupation of Hampton: General Magruder's order to burn the southern city to the

---

bars, 'points' and bends" of a river, see Mark Twain, *Life on the Mississippi* (Boston: J. R. Osgood, 1883), chapter 8.

ground. Here, as in other parts of his account, Wood's memory bends to suit local prejudices, as postwar recollection does its work in converting Confederate violence into something kindlier.[2] The officer who sparked Magruder's rage by showing him a newspaper article that depicted black families in white houses regrets the decision to do so, and Magruder was drunk when he gave the order. The entire episode comes close to ending peacefully as soldiers express their regret and fumble their way to Hampton—until the turpentine is poured on the houses. Wood goes on to describe the white families who became refugees in the burning of Hampton. And tellingly, he fails to record the fate of the black refugees who would settle there.[3]

Wood the river pilot gives his own post hoc discussion of the equally famous battle between the ironclads USS *Monitor* and CSS *Virginia* (or *Merrimack*), again demonstrating his specialized knowledge of rivers and ships. Recalling the encounter, he categorically states that the *Virginia* should not have driven its prow so forcefully into the wooden ship, the USS *Cumberland*. Had it pierced the *Cumberland* a little more gracefully, he asserts, the ironclad might have held back the rest of the Union navy and allowed other Confederate ships on the James River to enter the fight. Wood also declares confidently that the *Virginia* could not have been saved during the Confederate retreat toward Richmond in May of 1862, because the ironclad would

2. On war and memory, see Paul Fussell, *The Great War and Modern Memory* (New York: Oxford University Press, 1975); Nina Silber, *The Romance of Reunion: Northerners and the South, 1865–1900* (Chapel Hill: University of North Carolina Press, 1993); David W. Blight, *Race and Reunion: The Civil War in American Memory* (Cambridge, MA: Belknap Press of Harvard University Press, 2001); and W. Fitzhugh Brundage, *The Southern Past: A Clash of Race and Memory* (Cambridge, MA: Belknap Press of Harvard University Press, 2005).

3. On the burning of Hampton, see John V. Quarstein, *Hampton and Newport News in the Civil War: War Comes to the Peninsula* (Lynchburg, Va.: H.E. Howard, Inc., 1998), chapter 5.

have had to drop its guns to pass over the sandbars near Jamestown. And Wood knew precisely how deep the bars were.[4]

Many histories of the Civil War describe how slowly George McClellan's Union army moved up the Virginia peninsula, and its failure to capture Richmond in 1862—one of the perennial might-have-beens in most accounts of the war.[5] But few discuss the Union navy's difficulties in controlling the James River, and none with the fluency of George Wood. As Wood observes in his account of the Yankee fleet at City Point, the James was a vexing problem for the Union flotilla. Very few men knew the river well enough to steer steamers and schooners all the way to Richmond. In mid-May of 1862—after the Union army passed through Williamsburg, George tells us—he, his father, and the other James River pilots could have safely steered the Union steamers past the remaining obstructions and over the bars, putting the enemy ships safely behind Confederate defenses and close to Richmond. But the river pilots at City Point made the key decision not to help the Union ships steer past their town. Had they done so, Wood notes, the Confederates would not have had the chance to scuttle ships and sink them behind City Point, mount another gun on the bluffs, or man the batteries nearby. The Union navy might have driven on nearly to Richmond, Wood suggests, and the war might have ended in 1862.[6]

4. The most up-to-date telling of the encounter is Harold Holzer and Tim Mulligan, eds., *The Battle of Hampton Roads: New Perspectives on the USS* Monitor *and the CSS* Virginia (New York: Fordham University Press, co-published with the Mariners' Museum, 2006).

5. The most famous account is T. Harry Williams, *Lincoln and His Generals* (New York: Knopf, 1952). For the current debate see Gary W. Gallagher, ed., *The Richmond Campaign of 1862: The Peninsula and the Seven Days* (Chapel Hill: University of North Carolina Press, 2000).

6. There is a plethora of Civil War books that focus on the armies, but relatively few that consider armies and navies together. The most current

While diarists are always prepared to make their own experience seem critical and vital, the position of the river pilots speaks to a larger point about Union control of geography. Union ignorance of Southern geography bedeviled their occupation of the South throughout the war. Without up-to-date maps of land or water, their calculations relied on considerable guesswork. The Confederate high command, meanwhile, could readily organize the land- and waterscape to facilitate Confederate defenses. They flooded rivers like the Chickahominy, carefully calibrated the shape of defensive batteries, tested the range of artillery, and deployed underwater obstructions. Superior Union technology could not surmount the problem of poor geographical intelligence. Steamboats with metal bottoms, as Wood notes early in his account, could quickly founder in the James River without a good pilot to steer them. The men who knew the rocks and shoals, and could avoid them, mattered more than all the sophisticated engineering that the Union could muster.[7]

Wood also documents how this civil war could quickly turn uncivil. Early on, a young lady and a sea captain could negotiate about how a town was to be occupied, and hurrahs would break out in the neutral settlement of City Point and from the Yankee ships when a deal had been reached, with wisecracking songs echoing as ships were unloaded. But later, Wood describes a

---

account of the navies—a dual biography of Stephen R. Mallory and Gideon Welles, the Southern and Northern secretaries of the navy—is Jay W. Simson, *Naval Strategies of the Civil War: Confederate Innovations and Federal Opportunism* (Nashville, TN: Cumberland House, 2001).

7. On army fortifications, see Earl J. Hess, *Field Armies and Fortifications in the Civil War: The Eastern Campaigns, 1861–1864* (Chapel Hill: University of North Carolina Press, 2005). The history of naval fortifications has tended to focus on Vicksburg; see Ron Field, *American Civil War Fortifications (3): The Mississippi and River Forts* (Oxford: Osprey Publishing, 2007).

Confederate attack on a flag-of-truce boat in May of 1862, a clear violation of the rules of war. Union officers retaliated for this breach by firing warning shells over the town, as Union sailors broke into houses, using the Confederate breach as a pretext. "It was not safe after this to remain at City Point," Wood remarks. As the Wood family sought to negotiate the sharpening line between Union and Confederate, they found less and less neutral territory for them to traverse.[8]

Indeed, the line between battlefield and home front seemed to blur as the war progressed, especially after 1862, when the Wood family saw themselves as "gypsies," increasingly trying to find their way past Union lines to a place in the Confederacy. They discover that the first crop they plant in City Point is in an unsafe area and abandon it, and their next field becomes a scene of battle, as soldiers sleep in the midst of the wheat they have planted. The family of seven keep moving toward Richmond, stumbling over Union and Confederate pickets and (according to Wood) spotting Stonewall Jackson resting inside a tent and Robert E. Lee astride his sorrel horse.

Wood seeks some organizing framework to encompass the fear that he must have experienced as an unarmed civilian on a constantly-shifting battlefield. And indeed his discussion of other people's apprehensions seems calculated, even stereotyped. He describes how "colored" Old Aunt Eliza Atkins is terrified when the white boy Elisha Jenkins throws an oil jug down her chimney, noting that her "screams could be heard all over the village." He notes that Blassingham, a Williamsburg native who ordered a barrel of molasses that Wood found and

8. For a discussion of the shifting zones of occupation and the place of civilians, see Stephen V. Ash, *When the Yankees Came: Conflict and Chaos in the Occupied South, 1861–1865* (Chapel Hill: University of North Carolina Press, 1995).

appropriated, calls out surrender when he hears pigs moving through the bushes. And he catalogs a number of equally vivid responses. Jim Turner sings a brave song about being a soldier, but then drops to the earth when he hears a shell whiz overhead. A "young lady" who slept near the door of the Wood house "awoke with a scream" when a mule brayed near her face. "One of the darkies" on a boat receives a pipe full of gunpowder and is "frightened . . . nearly to death." Wood's sister Sally, resting near a feed house, finds the severed arm of a soldier near her that, George nonchalantly states, "frightened her badly." These stories of other people's fear—the reactions of black men, black women, white women, or "cowardly" men—become a way of revisiting terror through humor, as the humor simultaneously ridicules the person and minimizes the terror.

By comparison, Wood himself—and the Confederate soldiers, sailors, and officers he meets—seem to be fearless in the pages that follow. Charles Mallory walks on board a ship, "shoe deep with blood and brains." Wood's companions sail out to save a barge of Georgia soldiers. Stonewall Jackson ignores the shells bursting over him, and reminds a riding companion that "a good soldier never looks to the rear." Robert E. Lee, likewise is "every inch a soldier" with an "eagle eye." Nonetheless, Wood is too good an observer to ignore how this conflict crippled men, and recalls that Jackson's service in the Mexican War days left him with a crazy, creeping sensation in his arm, and that the final years of the Civil War made Lee gray, haggard, and fat.

These observations of fear and fearlessness are likely the vignettes that the mature Wood most often told and retold in the easy company of the barbershop or at Odd Fellows meetings. And they seem to have become more and more exaggerated with time. In the postwar years, as the cult of the Lost Cause, Jim Crow laws, and black disfranchisement become the order of the day, Wood may well have embellished, in equal measure, the fearlessness of Confederate soldiers and the fearfulness of black men, white women, and others he viewed as noncombatants.

Yet for all of his seeming self-assurance, Wood's own story shows him struggling to navigate waters he does not fully comprehend. By 1863 he has moved to the James River Canal. Here he well understands where the goods are going, and he describes the canal trade with colorful anecdotes. He grows more confident in an area controlled by Confederates, and becomes a devotee of the theater. He knows what desirables he and his "yellow" companion, Henry Richards, can sell as they shuttle other goods back and forth for the vessels plying the deeper water. But he is still a stranger to these ways and places: Richards must show him how to catch and eat a catfish, and Wood makes a rather bad navigator on a canal ark, as he is unable to respond quickly enough to the commands of a black cook who orders him when and how to turn. In short order, George becomes a mule tender.

Wood's position in all matters is complex, but especially with regard to race. He is angry at the black families who have occupied lots in the burned city of Hampton; he ridicules the lantern show about plantation days that black men present; and he often views black servants as objects of derision. Yet for all this he worked daily alongside Henry Richards, transporting goods for a Confederate quartermaster.

Most intriguing of all is the principal reason that young George plies the river dividing home front and battlefield: his father, Robert C. Wood. On the first reading we get the sense that George is a straight-up Confederate. He refers to Confederate soldiers as "our soldiers," and both he and his father are employed moving goods for the Confederate government. But we hear a few times that what prevents George's father from working for the Union is not his sympathies, but his oath and bond to the state. As a bonded river pilot, Robert C. Wood stood to lose a substantial sum *and* break an oath by working for the Union army. Many families that wrestled with Unionist sympathies faced this terrible choice: support the Confederacy or risk arrest.[9]

While George favored the Confederacy, the Wood family clearly argued about it. Indeed, Richmond Confederate authorities imprisoned Robert B. (George's older brother) for Union sympathies. From the concluding vignettes about him, it is possible that this older brother served as a spy for Allan Pinkerton's agency. One wonders if the Confederacy's burning of Hampton (and the Wood family house) angered George Wood, and helped push part of the family toward Unionism. In 1862, George's father goes to Richmond seeking his Unionist son, a move that draws the Wood family toward Richmond, into the heart of the Confederacy, and away from the advancing Union army. The Wood family's own conflicts over the Confederacy pulls George to waters he must negotiate carefully.

As the war drew to a close and Petersburg was enveloped in

9. On the position of Unionists in Richmond, see Elizabeth R. Varon, *Southern Lady, Yankee Spy: The True Story of Elizabeth Van Lew, a Union Agent in the Heart of the Confederacy* (New York: Oxford University Press, 2003). On Unionism generally in the South, see the articles in John C. Inscoe and Robert C. Kenzer, eds., *Enemies of the Country: New Perspectives on Unionists in the Civil War South* (Athens: University of Georgia Press, 2001). The fate of Unionists in Atlanta is described in Thomas G. Dyer, *Secret Yankees: The Union Circle in Confederate Atlanta* (Baltimore: Johns Hopkins University Press, 1999). Unionism in the Deep South is described in Margaret M. Storey, *Loyalty And Loss: Alabama's Unionists in the Civil War and Reconstruction* (Baton Rouge: Louisiana State University Press, 2004), and Victoria E. Bynum, *The Free State of Jones: Mississippi's Longest Civil War* (Chapel Hill: University of North Carolina Press, 2001). Unionism in coastal North Carolina is explored in Wayne K. Durrill, *War of Another Kind: A Southern Community in the Great Rebellion* (New York: Oxford University Press, 1990). A recent survey of Unionist sentiment throughout the South is David Williams, *Bitterly Divided: The South's Inner Civil War* (New York: New Press, 2008).

1864, the Woods determine to make their way back through Union lines. Here again, as in 1862, negotiations by a white woman protect the family from harm. George's sister Keturah speaks to General Hincks, telling him that her brother R.B. is a captive of the Confederacy and thereby gaining her safe passage back to Hampton. George, meanwhile, makes his way North past Union lines by finding a "yellow" blacksmith on good terms with Unionists, a biracial man who, like the "yellow" Henry Richards, is adept at manuvering between two worlds—black and white, free and slave—as well as the newly established boundary between Union and Confederate. Wood's familiarity with such men makes him a crosser of boundaries as well, and places him in peculiar danger: Confederate pickets might well mistake him for a soldier, and Union pickets at first wonder if he is a Union deserter. Well aware of such problems of identity, having crossed back and forth many times before, Wood carries a current Richmond newspaper with him to prove to the pickets that he has been in the Confederate capital, but that he has left the Confederacy behind. Sharing knowledge about Confederate trading routes makes him valuable to Union officers seeking to control their expanding lines.[10]

George Wood finished the war by establishing a mess, regularly preparing and eating his meals with other men in a blacksmith shop at Fort Monroe. Sometimes imprisoned, and at other times free to move about, they help rebuild Hampton from the ashes of the old city. But the postwar settlement still leaves much unsettled. Wood refers to free black men and women as "colored contrabands" whom he dared not insult. He

10. On the role of biracial men as border-crossers during the Civil War, see Scott Reynolds Nelson, "Red Strings and Half-Brothers: Civil War in Alamance County, North Carolina," in Inscoe and Kenzer, *Enemies of the Country.*

briefly describes the neighborhoods they built, including "Slabtown," a free community built of brick, clay, and wood in 1863. Hampton City finally tore the community down in the 1970s, ejecting its inhabitants.[11]

Wood lingers on a central conflict that will endure even after he is long gone: the citizenship of former slaves and their descendents in Virginia. President Andrew Johnson's plan for Reconstruction envisioned no place for black men and women in the postwar political order. In sharp opposition, Congress moved to reorganize the Southern states, in what came to be called Congressional Reconstruction. Virginia briefly became part of Military District Number One. The postwar Congress called for a constitutional convention in Virginia in which both black and white citizens would participate, and a newly ratified Fourteenth Amendment seemed to permanently guarantee equal voting rights. Congress backed up their commitment to black suffrage at first, threatening to negate the attempts of the Southern states to bar black men from the polls. Virginia public schools remained segregated, but the number of black schools increased considerably after the war.[12]

Nonetheless, Southern Democrats seemed determined to prevent black men from voting. In 1876, after Conservative Democrats had gained a substantial following among white voters, Virginia instituted a poll tax. The state's Republican Party paid the tax of those unable to do so. Thus in Wood's later

11. "Slabtown" appears to have followed the same trajectory as the black community in Yorktown; see Kelley Deetz, "Slabtown: Yorktown's African American Community, 1863–1970s" (honors thesis, College of William and Mary, 2002).

12. Richard M. Valelly, *The Two Reconstructions: The Struggle for Black Enfranchisement* (Chicago: University of Chicago Press, 2004), 56–59.

years, in the 1870s and 1880s, black political participation in Virginia remain relatively high.[13]

But in 1900, Wood and other Southerners finally got their way. In that year, Virginia Democrats pushed through a "grandfather clause" that limited voting to the descendents of those who had voted in 1860. Over thirty years of African American progress seemed doomed to failure.[14] The date of 1860 had symbolic significance, as this blocked those voters whose fathers and grandfathers had been slaves, but also reminded all at the polls of Virginia's secession. That particular vote had been a bitterly contested one, forcing Unionists to submit to war when Governor Henry Wise laid his pistol on the podium at the convention and told them that Virginia's militia was already firing at Union troops.[15] In the years since secession and war, postwar memoirs took Virginia's fraught and complex journey and made it seem inevitable. Reenactments of the Civil War, along with recollections of the "dark days" of Reconstruction that echo Wood's account, actually served to justify black disfranchisement and the rise of Jim Crow, despite the fact that Virginia's period under Congressional Reconstruction was very short.[16] Issues of race and reunion changed; racial views hardened.[17]

13. Ibid.

14. See Michael Perman, *Struggle for Mastery: Disfranchisement in the South, 1888–1908* (Chapel Hill: University of North Carolina Press, 2001).

15. See Scott Reynolds Nelson and Carol Sheriff, *A People at War: Civilians and Soldiers in America's Civil War, 1854–1877* (New York: Oxford University Press, 2007), chapter 2.

16. On the way that Southern Democrats used memories of Reconstruction to justify disfranchisement, see Bruce E. Baker, *What Reconstruction Meant: Historical Memory in the American South* (Charlottesville: University of Virginia Press, 2007).

17. On the "memory war" that followed the Civil War, see Blight, *Race and Reunion*.

After his father died, George Wood made one final transition in the postwar years. As he grew older he moved from the son and brother of a Unionist to something akin to a Confederate, with a story as hypnotic and fluid as the river he made his living on.

Editor's Note and Acknowledgments

George Randolph Wood did not grow up on a rural farm, as did most boys his age in Virginia at the onset of the Civil War. He lived in Hampton, a seaport that evolved from an English settlement of 1610 to become a small yet stable commercial center for farmers and oystermen, and the seat of Elizabeth City County. Located on the stubby and relatively shallow Hampton River, the city looked out on the expansive harbor known as Hampton Roads—as did its more cosmopolitan neighbors on Old Point Comfort, the federal garrison of Fort Monroe, and a popular resort hotel, the Hygeia. Schooners and steamboats from Norfolk and from wharfs all along the shore of the Chesapeake Bay docked daily at Hampton and the deepwater pier at Old Point.

A geographical and statistical description of Hampton published in 1856 reports the citizenry supported eighteen stores and four churches. There were two prominent boarding schools, Chesapeake Female College and the Hampton Male and Female Academy, the latter administered with a supplementary military curriculum by militia Major John Baytop Cary. There was also a militia regiment on call to apprehend runaway slaves.

Hampton had a population of about 1,200 residents in 1860, and prominent among them were at least two dozen harbor pilots. George Wood's father piloted ships through Capes Charles and Henry to harbors in Hampton Roads, as had both of his grandfathers.

The Wood family lived in the Pee Dee neighborhood, bound by the river and within a few blocks of the city's center, the crossroads of King and Queen streets. Families were large and several were connected by marriage, especially those of harbor pilots, whose economic success depended on co-ownership of schooners and mutual adherence to the traditions and rules of their profession.

George Wood was raised in a large, tight-knit family, and in a community shaped by constant interaction with outsiders—mariners, soldiers, and travelers on business and holiday. Hampton was not a provincial Southern city. Nevertheless, it was, by law and by custom, a segregated society. No member of the Wood family, however, owned slaves, according to census tabulations.

After the election of Abraham Lincoln in 1860, the people of Hampton initially had no need and little inclination to be caught up in the secessionist movement. However, communal allegiance shifted suddenly and dramatically from the nation to the state in mid-April 1861, as Union soldiers filled Fort Monroe's barracks and Union warships blockaded Hampton Roads.

Harbor pilots held state warrants, and with the war's arrival they lost their authority. Many, including the family headed by Robert Clement Wood, George's father, fled the martial tension in the streets to sanctuary up the James River. Two of George Wood's older brothers enlisted in a Virginia regiment. His oldest brother, Robert B. Wood, stayed behind; he was a Union sympathizer.

For a year, the family lived at City Point, at the confluence of the Appomattox and James rivers. With his father, George Wood—who was fourteen years old—worked for the Confederacy aboard a supply ship transporting military cargo to troops manning defensive positions along the James River.

In May 1862, when a Union fleet arrived at City Point, the family first evacuated across the James to Charles City County and then through military lines and over the corpse-strewn battlefield at Malvern Hill to Richmond, the capital of the Confederacy.

George and his father were assigned a transport barge on the James River and Kanawha Canal above Richmond, but his father, who was in his late fifties, grew weary and returned with his wife and children to City Point to live in a crowded mansion on the bank of the Appomattox. When a Union division of African American soldiers arrived early in May 1864, the Wood family retreated under the protection of Federal officers to Hampton, which lay in ruins.

All this time, George Wood continued to work on the tidal waterways, transporting cargo in barges towed by steam-powered tugs or pushed by poles and aided by currents and tides. It was heavy labor, often shared with a black companion, Henry Richards, whose status—free man or enslaved—is unknown.

George saw artillery shells descend in his direction, swapped stories with Hampton boys in military encampments, and twice witnessed Robert E. Lee in the field. He went hungry—and he sampled caviar. There was danger and deprivation; still, when he was in Richmond he attended theatrical performances whenever he could.

After he learned of his father's death in Hampton, George decided to return there to be with his mother. He teamed up with a fellow barge captain who wanted to get to New York—a man identified only as Cullory—and in October 1864 sneaked past Confederate guards and surrendered to Federal authorities east of Richmond. He formally swore allegiance to the United States and was given steamer passage home. After a period of detention, he found work with a blacksmith outside Fort Monroe.

This is the stuff of adventure—the experiences of a young man held fresh in his memory for forty years, when at last he wrote them down. George Wood randomly filled at least five journal books with personal remembrances, stories he heard from family members, and episodes of Virginia's colonial era he copied from history books. Two of Wood's journals, along with some family papers, have been entrusted to the Library of the Mariners' Museum, in Newport News, with enlarged photocopies generously provided by Susan Berg, the museum's former vice president and librarian, and her library staff. Three other journals are owned by the city of Hampton and preserved by the Hampton History Museum, where the curator, J. Michael Cobb, graciously made them available.

It is with their permission and the encouragement and generous sponsorship of Dorothy Rouse-Bottom of the William E. Rouse Library in Hampton, that I undertook the task of compiling, editing, and publishing George Wood's recollections of his Civil War experiences, which comprise only a portion of his scrawled journal entries.

Wood wrote during the first decade of the twentieth century, when Lost Cause sentiment, influenced by daily association with older veterans, worked to soften his memory of the harsh and harrowing events he witnessed. He favors telling lighter moments of wartime incidents and relates them in a terse, nonflowery style.

It must be acknowledged, however, that his writing is often repetitious, and his reiterations offer both corroborative and additional details, and leave minor variances to be sorted out.

In order to corroborate and correct the factual information—names, dates, places, and the like—in Wood's journal books, I have consulted standard and local references, which are listed in the bibliography.

Of principal help were two reminiscences attributed to Wood's younger sister, Emma Wood Richardson. One is a typescript of her handwritten "Notes on the Civil War" that was made in 1959 by Thelma P. Savage, a copy of which is in the Library of Virginia in Richmond. Thelma Savage is the granddaughter of Edwin "Ned" Hicks Wood, a brother of both George

Wood and Emma Wood Richardson. The other reminiscence by Emma Wood Richardson is a newspaper article published anonymously in the weekly "Confederate Column" of the *Richmond Times-Dispatch.* A clipping of this article, published on November 29, 1908, is pasted in George Wood's journal with a marginal attribution to "Emma, Mrs. J. W. Richardson." Extensive citations from both these memoirs have been used to annotate George Wood's account of the family fleeing from Charles City County to Richmond in 1862 and leaving Weston Manor near City Point and returning to Hampton in 1864.

George Wood wrote hurriedly and was apt to change topics abruptly, sometimes in the middle of a paragraph. He didn't always adhere to rules of punctuation, capitalization, and spelling. He wrote "enouf" for enough and, oddly, "Brittish" for British. Misspellings and occasional lapses in punctuation have been corrected silently for the ease of modern readers. However, in some selected instances, I have avoided adding such corrections to retain a flavor of Wood's writing. Where words, phrases, dates, or brief explanatory text were inserted for purposes of clarity, they are identified with brackets. Wood's frequent use of parentheses has been retained. Footnotes identify unfamiliar terms, provide discursive explanations of salient points, and incorporate additional passages of Wood's text into his account.

When introducing persons, or in listing groups of persons, Wood often relies on initials rather than full first names, even when referring to his father as R. C. Wood. Occasionally, George Wood mentions himself in the third person, G. R. Wood.

Whatever military or honorific rank that Wood assigns to men has been left in place. Readers should be aware that Wood tends to use the highest military rank that the individuals portrayed were awarded, and not necessarily the rank held at the time when the person is encountered.

Some geographical features of Tidewater Virginia that Wood cites—both natural and man-made—have changed over the years, and a few have disappeared. Wherever possible, the locations of Civil War–era places have been identified and mapped to allow readers to follow George Wood's extensive travels. The inconsistent use of an apostrophe in names of landmarks is deliberate and reflects Wood's usage, as well as identifications found on nineteenth-century maps.

Wood recites extensive lyrics of songs he heard and sang, but does not indicate if he wrote them from memory or copied them from an unidentified songbook. In either case, a review of Civil War verse confirms the song titles, while documentation of all the lyrics remains elusive. Books that Wood mentions have been verified, and are included in the bibliography.

The challenges of reviving and restoring the Civil War portion of George Wood's journal has been immeasurably helped by Theresa Hammond, whose research unearthed answers to puzzling questions and who drew together the illustrations; by Sharon Garrison, who compiled the index; and by Susan Berg, who advised on preparation of the text for publication. All three are affiliated with Port Hampton Press, of which Dorothy Rouse-Bottom is publisher. Maps were drawn by William L. Nelson of Accomac, Virginia.

Scott Nelson—an award-winning historian, Legum Professor of History at the College of William and Mary, and co-author of *A People at War: Civilians and Soldiers in America's Civil War*—brings his extensive knowledge of how average Americans coped with war in their midst to his insightful interpretation of George Wood's memory and writing.

This project is indebted to George Wood's granddaughter, Jacqueline Gaylord Milliken of Hampton, for her encouragement and personal insight into the Wood family. She fondly remembers her grandfather bouncing her on his knee when she was a youngster. Mrs. Milliken's daughter, Jacqueline Powers Park, also of Hampton, graciously lent her assistance.

The validity of George Wood's writing was affirmed and enhanced by J. Michael Moore, historian at Lee Hall Mansion in Newport News, who read the prepublication text and offered comments, suggestions, and a correction or two. His knowledge of the Civil War in Virginia is encyclopedic, and he proved it by pointing out that Wood incorrectly recalled that Robert E. Lee had only a mustache when he saw him in 1862, because the general grew a beard while campaigning in western Virginia in 1861.

Several other historians and reference librarians willingly responded to inquiries and filled gaps of explanatory information. Among them are Carol Kittenburg Dubbs of Williamsburg, author of *Defend This Old Town: Williamsburg During the Civil War;* Shelby Liston of Hampton, historian of the Veterans Administration Hospital in Hampton; Claudia A. Jew, director of Photographic Services, Licensing, and Publications for the Mariners' Museum in Newport News; Judith F. Ledbetter, director of the Charles City County Historical Society; John M. Coski, librarian and historian at the Museum of the Confederacy in Richmond; and Mary Sawyer Molineux, reference librarian at the Earl Gregg Swem Library at the College of William and Mary.

With their persistent assistance, George Wood's compelling story of navigating tidal currents as well as shifting political and societal allegiances is recounted in the pages that follow, to be appreciated and remembered. His experiences as a teenager on Confederate waterways are both unique and revealing, as he may be the only Virginia boatman to write of them.

Will Molineux
March 2009

Chronology

1847

November 7 George Randolph Wood is born in Hampton to Robert Clement and Susan Davis Hicks Wood.

1859

October 16–18 John Brown's raid on Harper's Ferry to incite a slave insurrection is put down.

1861

February 22 George Wood witnesses the presentation of a flag to the Wythe Rifles of the 115th Militia Regiment.

April 12 The Civil War begins, as Confederate artillery opens fire on Fort Sumter in Charleston Harbor, South Carolina.

April 17 Virginia's Secession Convention adopts an Ordinance of Secession to leave the Union by a vote of 88 to 55.

April 19 President Abraham Lincoln orders the blockade of all ports in the Confederate states, an order that is extended to Hampton Roads.

April 20 Virginia militiamen parade in Hampton.

April 20–21 Union forces destroy Gosport (Norfolk) Navy Yard and sink the frigate USS *Merrimack;* Confederates later salvage the yard, raise the hull, and use it to build the ironclad CSS *Virginia.*

April 23 The family of Robert C. Wood evacuates Hampton aboard the pilot boat, *Plume.*

April 25 or 26 The Wood family arrives at City Point and settles in "a large brick house."

May 13–14 Young men in Hampton, many of them students of John Cary's Military Academy, enlist in militia units such as the Wythe Rifles and Old Dominion Dragoons.

May 23 Virginians ratify the Ordinance of Secession by a vote of 132,207 to 37,451. The vote in Hampton is 360 to 6. Union troops from Fort Monroe march into downtown Hampton as a show of force and return to the post.

May 24 Union General Benjamin F. Butler declares three slaves—Jim Townsend, Isaac Monroe, and Frank Baker (who have run away from Colonel Charles K. Mallory of Hampton and are seeking sanctuary in Fort Monroe)—to be contraband of war.

June 10 The Battle of Big Bethel is fought outside Hampton.

August 7 The city of Hampton is burned by Confederate Militia.

September 15 Robert C. Wood takes command of the transport schooner *James Buchanan* and George Wood signs on as a deckhand.

1862

March 8–9 The Battle of the Ironclads (also known as the Battle of Hampton Roads), between the USS *Monitor* and CSS *Virginia* (formerly the USS *Merrimack*), takes place in Hampton Roads.

April 2 General George McClellan arrives at Fort Monroe in command of the Army of the Potomac for the Peninsula Campaign.

May 4 Robert and George Wood arrive in Richmond after retreating up the James River from Kingsmill Wharf. A few days later their vessel is used to build a pontoon bridge, and the Woods row from Richmond to City Point.

May 5 The Battle of Williamsburg is fought east of the city. Afterwards both armies move up the Peninsula and form lines to the east of Richmond in advance of the Seven Days Campaign.

May 11 The CSS *Virginia* is scuttled off Craney Island.

May 13 Union gunboats, including the USS *Monitor*, arrive at City Point.

May 15 The Union fleet (including the USS *Monitor* and the

USS *Galena*) is repulsed at the Battle of Drewry's Bluff and returns to City Point.

May 19 A Union physician and naval officers, while on a humanitarian mission ashore at City Point, are taken captive by Confederates.

Later in May The family of Robert C. Wood leaves City Point and crosses the James River to Eppes Island, taking up residence in "a house near Rowland's Mill" in Charles City County.

July 1 The Battle of Malvern Hill, Charles City County, ends the Seven Days Campaign, and the Army of the Potomac establishes camp at Berkeley Plantation.

Later in July The family of Robert C. Wood evacuates to Richmond and initially lives in a house rented by G. B. West.

Late July or August Robert C. Wood is given command of a canal boat on the James River and Kanawha Canal, with George accompanying him.

August George Wood leaves the canal boat and finds temporary work at the Richmond docks.

Late summer George Wood is given command of a large tobacco ark and begins to transport freight between Richmond and wharfs along the James River. When in Richmond, George Wood frequently attends the theater.

1863

August 5 George Wood sees the damaged USS *Commodore Barney* being towed down the James River past Shirley Plantation.

Fall Robert C. Wood moves his family from Richmond to Weston Manor on the Appomattox River.

1864

February George Wood visits Weston.

April 30 George Wood's nephew, George Cake, is born at Weston.

May 5 The Union Army of the James under General Benjamin Butler lands at Bermuda Hundred without opposition, and General Edward W. Hincks, in command of a division of African American troops, occupies City Point.

Mid-May George Wood is hemmed in with his ark at Petersburg. Robert C. Wood and his family evacuate Weston and, under the protection of General Hincks, return by steamship to Hampton.

June 7 Robert C. Wood, George's father, dies in Hampton and is buried in St. John's Church Cemetery.

June 14–16 General Ulysses S. Grant's army, advancing toward Petersburg, crosses the James River from Wilcox's Wharf in Charles City County to Windmill Point in Prince George County.

June 15 General Grant establishes his headquarters in Appomattox Manor at City Point.

June 18 General Robert E. Lee arrives in Petersburg.

Late June George Wood abandons his ark and returns to Richmond, and later returns to duty transporting supplies to Confederate forts at Drewry's and Chaffin's bluffs.

October 18 George Wood leaves Richmond for Hampton.

Late October George Wood arrives at Fort Monroe where, after being confined briefly, he rejoins his family in Hampton and finds work at Fort Monroe.

November 7 George Wood claims to have voted for President Lincoln in an apparent mock presidential election.

1865

April 3 News of the surrender of Richmond is celebrated at Fort Monroe.

1872

December 26 Susan Davis Hicks Wood, George Wood's mother, dies in Hampton and is buried in St. John's Church Cemetery.

1883

April 5 George Wood marries Annie Lee Bryon in Hampton.

1920

December 7 George Wood dies in Hampton and is buried in St. John's Church Cemetery.

A Young Virginia Boatman Navigates the Civil War

73

Was made by driving piles putting heavy caps acrost running Screws through them from peaces at bottom thus 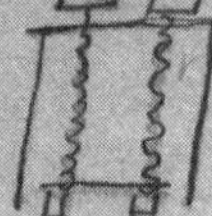 After getting through with Job Capt Airtis Who was manager of Water transpotation under Maj Kensey Johns Son of Bishop Johns gave me Command of a large Ark Called Jno Letcher - While Capt Joe S Was put on the Wm L Goggin These boats Were during the Canvas for Govener When Letcher Was elected in 1859 or 1860 they Were Sharp head and Square Stern So as to put the Stern to the Wharf load With flower or Tobacco And also to rolle th on board of Ships - Richmond had a large trade to Bre Germany for tobacco and trade to Brazil With flo When the Arks Were built - Ships Would take a part of their load in Richmond and drophed down the beyond the Bars in the river and these Arks Wo be loaded and towed down to them So they Could finish loading. Our first Work With the Arks Was to raise the Tidely Idely whose true na Was Junius A. Brown Which We did under Supervision of Mr Gill & Mr Booker City officers assisted by Master Workman Fox. We Swch chains under her and fastened them to beams acrost ou decks at low Water and When the tide arose Steamer Was lifted. We only had one men b our Selfs on each Ark. My first trip Was to Rock or Howlets or Pull and be damned for load of Wood arrived there about 12 o clock and Went to See Mr Howlett Who invited me in the a large

George R. Wood's Family

"Father Was a Harbor Pilot"

George Randolph Wood's maternal great-grandfather, John Hicks, owned a marine railway along the Hampton River on a broad point of land he called Pee Dee, named perhaps for an ancestral home in England. By the mid-nineteenth century, Pee Dee was a neighborhood where sea captains and harbor pilots lived and where John Cary's Hampton Military Academy fronted the river. Here is where George Randolph Wood grew up in the decade before the outbreak of the Civil War.

Wood's father and an uncle were pilots of sailing ships in Virginia's busy port of Hampton Roads, as had been both of his grandfathers. He was the tenth of twelve children born to Robert Clement and Susan Davis Hicks Wood. When George filled the pages of his bound journal books with personal recollections early in the twentieth century, he did not list his siblings in order of their birth, and omitted his oldest sister, Mary Jane, who died when he was five years old. He did specifically note one nephew, Jefferson Wingfield, orphaned during the Civil War and raised by his unmarried sister and who, along with George and members of his immediate family, were well-known residents of postwar Hampton.

I was born in Hampton in the part that is called Pee Dee[1] on the afternoon of November 7, 1847. About 4 o'clock my Mother looked out of the east window across Hampton River

1. Pee Dee is the Hampton neighborhood between Eaton Street, known as Hospital Street in the eighteenth and nineteenth centuries, and the Hampton River below Pee Dee Cove. Hampton, the major seaport on the Peninsula, was the seat of rural Elizabeth City County. Clusters of farmers and oystermen lived in the neighborhoods of Fox Hill and Back River, and out-

at a lighter[2] being rowed up the river containing the remains of old Mrs. Ward. I do not remember like Captain Brown or King David, who they say [could] remember events that happened years before they were born, and did not see the funeral cortege or witness her burial at the graveyard near Mr. A. S. Segar's house, but was told of it, and I was born just two hours afterwards.

My father was Robert C. Wood, born in August 1804, a Virginia harbor pilot,[3] the son of James Wood, also a pilot. My mother was Susan Hicks, born in December 1808. Mother was the daughter of William Hicks, a pilot. Mother was dark while Father was medium light-complexioned.

Father and mother were married early in life—he at 22, she at 16 years old. They had Emma Virginia and Martha, [both] light after Father; Robert B. and John B., after Mother's shade; William, after Father's; Keturah, Elizabeth, and Sallie, after Mother; Sam B., George Randolph, and Edward Hicks, after Father's complexion.[4]

Elizabeth married in 1858 and died in 1861 at City Point leaving one son, Jefferson [Wingfield].

Father was a very strong man and a large one. On one occa-

---

side Fort Monroe on Old Point Comfort. The county's population in 1860 was 5,798 (3,180 whites, 201 free black, 2,417 enslaved).

2. A barge-like vessel used to load or unload ships at anchor offshore; also known as a receiving vessel.

3. Captains whose profession it is to guide vessels into or out of port or within river channels. Prior to the Civil War, pilots were licensed by the Commonwealth of Virginia to serve Hampton Roads and to navigate the Rappahannock and James rivers.

4. George Wood doesn't list his siblings in order of age; Emma Virginia was the youngest and Martha the oldest. Other than that, he identifies them in order of birth. A brother, named Allen, apparently born after William and before Keturah, died in infancy. As George Wood notes, several of his brothers have the middle initial *B,* but he gives no full name.

sion while hunting in the Bates Woods, now where the Electric Road passes to Newport News, he saw a large Negro man up a tree. The Negro was a runaway from his master. By threatening the Negro with a load of shot, he made him come down from the tree and march in front of him. When the path got narrow he turned on father, seized the gun and endeavored to wrench it out of his hands, but father held on with one hand and struck him a blow with the other hand that fell him to the ground, then bound him with his suspender and brought him to Hampton and lodged him in jail. There was a $2 reward for his capture, but father was good natured and since the man was owned by a poor widow, he did not claim the reward.

Father and mother were both strict members of the Baptist Church having been baptized in 1842. He was a deacon at one time.

Father endured many hardships at sea before the war began between the states. The pilots in those days were not in an association like now and each boat made what it could out of the business. They cruised well out to sea and their boats were from twenty-five to fifty tons while those of today are several hundred tons. They were smart sailors used to handling all kinds of vessels—[whether] square-rigged or "fore and after,"[5] but only a few of them were educated enough to navigate a ship [on the open sea].

In 1840 father was in the pilot boat *Relief* [when it was] blown off shore in a gale and remained in the Gulf Stream and was supposed to be lost. Much anxiety was felt for the safety of the pilots and prayers were offered in the churches every night for

5. A vessel rigged with fore-and-aft sails designed to have a leading edge (luff) and a trailing edge (leech), cut in a triangular or quadrilateral shape. Most small craft have fore-and-aft sails because they are more versatile than square sails.

three weeks, but they finally got back safe. When they got in, the Negroes ran from them as they thought they were ghosts.

He was a Union man and opposed to slavery, but when the state cast her fortune with the seceding states and commerce stopped, he, along with the other pilots, offered their services to Gov. John Letcher. He went through the war until June 1864 enduring many hardships and having to move often. He and I served nearly all the time in the government transportation service. About one year we served together.

He returned home [in May 1864], after getting past Union lines the second time, and died one month later of cholera, making mother a widow until 1872 when she died of paralysis. Father was sixty years at death and mother sixty-four years. She lived to see me an Odd Fellow and Mason and member of her church. Father was a member of Patrick Henry Lodge of Odd Fellows. He knew many naval officers and was treated during the war on both sides with the greatest courtesy.

Evacuating to City Point

"A Dark Foreboding"

John Brown's 1859 raid on Harper's Ferry sent shock waves across Virginia, and in Hampton the militia company, the Wythe Rifles, enforced a curfew of all blacks while harbor pilots monitored their passage aboard ships. Prominent men organized a cavalry unit, the Old Dominion Dragoons, and an artillery battery, the Washington Artillery, both within the surveillance of Union forces at Fort Monroe.

When the Virginia Secession Convention voted to secede, militia officers positioned lookouts to monitor the U.S. military buildup at Fort Monroe and the blacks seeking refuge there. In a moment of bravura, one lieutenant sang a popular marching tune with words taken from a poem by Robert Burns.

Harbor pilots abandoned their lingering Union sympathies, and Robert C. Wood and the other co-owners of the pilot ship *Plume* took their families to safety up the James River, expecting to be away just a short time. At Jamestown, two nieces of George Wood, Harriet and Josephine Wingfield, were sent to live in Williamsburg. The Wood family paid a sentimental visit to Claremont, where they once lived when Robert Wood was a river pilot, before settling at City Point.

In reciting these events, George Wood paused to comment on William Allen, the wealthiest man in Virginia (who owned Jamestown Island and extensive properties along the James River), and on Allen's treatment of slaves, and to defend, in retrospect, the actions of a U.S. naval officer related to a prominent Hampton family.

During a peaceful interlude in City Point, George and some rambunctious pals frolicked along the riverbank and played a cruel prank on "Old Aunt Eliza Atkins." Meanwhile, two of George's older brothers, John and William, served with the Thirty-second Virginia Infantry Regiment at Yorktown, and another brother, Robert, was imprisoned in Richmond as a Union spy.

It was during the state of cheerful antebellum times that the Wythe Rifles were organized in 1857 with the following officers: W. R. Willis, captain; Thomas Latimer, first lieutenant; S. R. Chisman, second lieutenant; James Dye, third lieutenant; John Moore, fourth lieutenant; Dr. William Jennings, surgeon; F. A. Schmelz, quartermaster; S. W. Armistead, first sergeant; John Saunders, second sergeant; J. C. Lieford, third sergeant; Robert Cary Mahone, fourth sergeant; S. J. White, color sergeant.

The Wythe Rifles was Hampton's third militia company. The first was the Lafayette Guards, which marched to Yorktown in 1824 to receive General [Marquis de] Lafayette. The second was the Light Infantry Guards which often paraded through the streets with Professor Pedro Giacchetti leading the Old Point Band.

The John Brown insurrection in 1859 caused much excite-

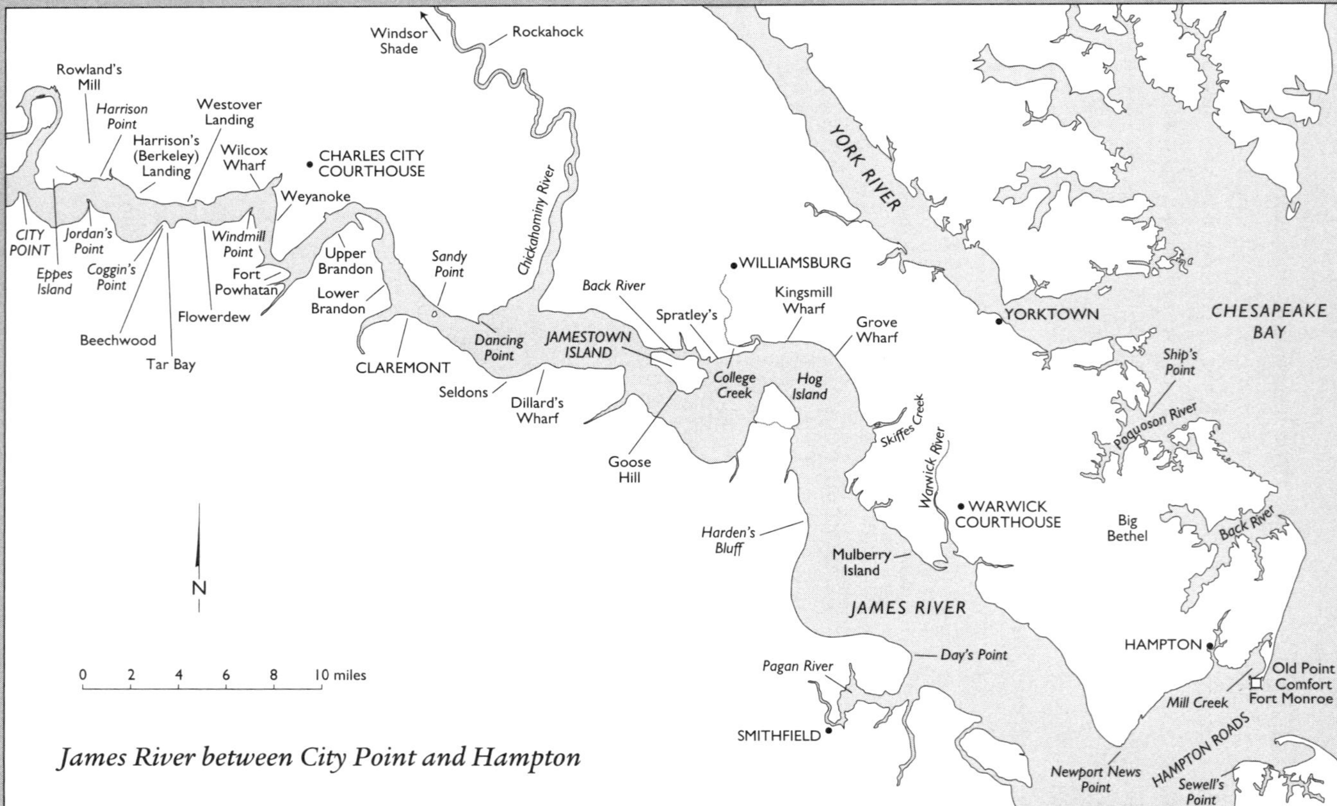

James River between City Point and Hampton

ment and increased the ever constant dread of the slaves rising in insurrection. Patrols would be started out almost every night. The Wythe Rifles, [then] the only organized volunteer company here, offered its services to Gov. [Henry A.] Wise, but were not accepted as others were nearer [Harper's Ferry].

The patrols required all colored people without a pass to be in at the toll of the bells 9 o'clock and many of them would be chased and, if caught, locked in jail. If they had a bag of corn or meal, the town sergeant, Mr. [Fred] Palmer, would confiscate it.

The legislature had passed an act that all vessels bound north should be inspected to prevent carrying away our slaves. The pilots were required as warrant officers of the state to execute this law and one of the pilot boats each month was put on inspection [duty] with a brass 12-pound gun on her bow. The Wythe Rifles would be sent for to board the vessels that resisted the search.

On February 22, 1861, the Wythe Rifles paraded and were drawn up in a line in front of Mr. Cary's [Military] Academy. John Cary, the principal, was especially adapted for teaching and he had an able corps of teachers. He had about 200 scholars, day and boarders, and many of those students were able soldiers and officers during the Civil War, and some of them filled soldiers' graves.

The cause of the parade was the presentation of a flag by Capt. James Hicks to the 115th Militia Regiment and, as this was the only volunteer organized company of the regiment, the Rifles were to receive it. Mr. Baker P. Lee, now Major Lee, made the presentation and Captain [William Royall] Willis received it on behalf of the company. This flag is now in possession of his son, John M. Willis.

The company [of Wythe Rifles] was Company A in 32nd Regiment when the war began. The company was [made up of] fine drilled soldiers who were serviceable before the war began.

Their uniform was dark blue with green trimming, green epaulets, worsted green cord down the pants, frock coats, black hats pinned up at the side, black feathers. Officers had gold trimming with black hats, white feathers. When the war began they were well drilled even in the skirmish and bayonet exercises in [William J.] Hardee's *Rifle and Light Infantry Tactics.*

The company paraded once a month and Mr. [Francis Anton] Schmelz gave a silver cup for best shot, which was won by James T. Outten. A banquet followed. A second target practice for a plume and sword [was held] and the plume was won by Sergeant Mahone and sword went to Sergeant Tilford. The Wythe Rifles had many parades headed by the O. P. [Old Point] Band and the music of "Old Kentucky Home," "Annie Lourie" will be long remembered.[6]

6. Elsewhere, George Wood says the Wythe Rifles "drilled nightly in the old Syms Eaton Academy—house at night, yard in day or on Courthouse Green."

In an undated letter to the *Richmond Times-Dispatch,* published circa 1905 and pasted in a journal book, Wood writes:

> When the militia assembled at the courthouse yard in the spring of 1861 flintlock muskets were issued to many of the men. One old Fox Hiller said: "This is a h— of a weapon to go to war with," and while passing over a bridge, threw the antiquated fowling piece in the stream below. Arriving at Ship Point, the sergeant was ordered to drill the men in the manual of arms, but as part of the men were supplied with percussion cap guns and part with flintlocks, he said he would have to separate the two because Hardee's *Tactics* for flintlock guns gave twelve movements in loading and only nine for percussion cap guns. They were also drilled in file and section movements.
>
> Critics might say that our men, having been raised so near Fort Monroe and having a chance to witness the drilling of the regulars in that fortification, should have made good soldiers, walking erect with their heads and shoulders up, treading on their heels and not their toes as though they were treading clams; body not drooping over as though they were plowing, but straight and head and shoulders not shaking as though they were holding a courts-martial.

All these military preparations were very exciting to a young boy of thirteen years old. I would follow a drum and fife from Mill Creek [through Hampton] to Big Bethel, but after four years of the war [I] would not cross the street to see a regimental parade with the marine band at its head.

When the company heard that Governor Wise was on his way to the Eastern Shore the company assembled to act as his escort, boarded the steamer and sent to the fort for the drum and fife corps, which came on at Old Point—the last music they got from there.

The Old Dominion Dragoons were organized and afterwards fought gallantly through the war as Company B, 3rd Virginia Cavalry. The following were the officers: J. C. Phillips, captain; W. R. Vaughan, first lieutenant; Gill Cary, second lieutenant; G. Booker Jones, third lieutenant; Fayette Sinclair, W. T. Smith, William N. Causey, and George J. Smith, sergeants; S. W. Phillips, Jas. B. White, Jos. B. Herbert and Gilbert Phillips, corporals.

Next came the organization of our artillery company, to be called the Washington Artillery, with C. L. Smith, captain; G. William Semple and William Fraser, first lieutenants; Dr. Jesse P. Hope and Thomas Tabb, second lieutenants. [They wore a] dark blue uniform, red trimming.

The company got a 12-pound brass gun when the Federals evacuated Portsmouth Navy Yard. Mr. Buchanan made a carriage for it and it did fine execution at Seven Pines [May 31–June 1, 1862, east of Richmond]. They had no arms except a short cutlass; the boys called these cheese knives. These were discarded as artillery did not fight with anything but their cannon.

The company was stationed the first year at Ship Point. This is the point [in York County] made by the Poquoson River and Chisman Creek. The company elected new officers after the first year and part of the company was dissatisfied when the company disbanded. Some went to other commands while the

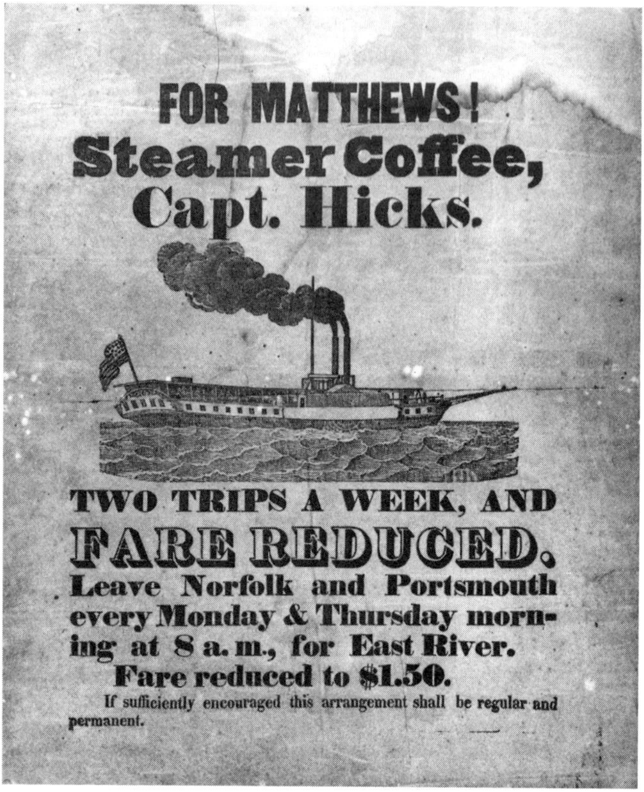

Prewar advertisement for the steamer *J. E. Coffee*. (Mariners' Museum)

bulk of them went to Carter's Battery [of the King William Artillery] and did valiant service.

We knew that good times around Hampton was getting scarce. We were too near a strong fort to attack it by land with the [Union] navy against us. The old commandant [of Fort Monroe] was Col. [Justin] Dimick, who mounted guns on the land side to be prepared for any attack.

The steamer *J. E. Coffee* came over from Norfolk one night and took on the Wythe [Rifles] and went down to capture the lightship. They could not get up the anchor and the ship, being iron bottom, could not get a hole in her to sink the ship so had to leave her at her station. It was well they did as lighted lanterns were going all around the [fort's] ramparts as though they were getting ready to fire on the *Coffee.*

On Saturday, [April 20],[7] the four companies paraded with a band from Norfolk as the Old Point Band was not allowed up. About 1 o'clock the parade halted in front of the present post office just in front of E. G. Darden's residence on King Street. A brick building stood there used as a bar. Speeches were made by Capt. [William Royall] Willis, Lt. [Thomas S.] Latimer, John Moore, J. Barron Hope, Captain [Charles L.] Smith, Dr. William R. Vaughan and Lt. Thomas Tabb.

Tabb said, "I hold in my hand an order as officer of the day to place a guard at Old Point or Mill Creek and one at Dennis' place to prevent the slaves from running away to General Butler at Old Point." Dennis had a wharf at Blackbeard's Point opposite the [Chesapeake] Female College (now Soldiers Home) and a store on the said wharf.

He quoted Jamie Brown at Luckner: "Dinna yea hear the slogan the Campbells are coming?"

The steamers *J. E. Coffee,* Norfolk, Capt. Pat McCormick, and the *Northampton,* [which served] Mathews and the Eastern Shore, Capt. James Hicks, had stopped running. Colonel Dimick, a stern military officer, was in command at Fort Monroe. He had his spies all around pretending to be men anxious to desert.

The Federals set fire to the Portsmouth [Gosport] Navy Yard

7. Three days earlier, on April 17, the Virginia Secession Convention in Richmond had adopted an ordinance to leave the Union by a vote of 88 to 55. Charles K. Mallory, a prominent Hampton attorney, was elected to represent Elizabeth City and adjoining jurisdictions on the Peninsula in the convention and signed the Ordinance of Secession, which Virginia voters ratified on May 23 by a vote of 132,207 to 37,451.

Saturday night [April 20]. The old battleship *Pennsylvania,* drawing 28 feet of water and used as a receiving [vessel] for years, *Merrimack,* and other vessels were burnt. The frigate *Cumberland* and the steamer *Pawnee* came down to Sewell's Point and anchored to blockade the river. The Sunday night was a beautiful sight with the warships anchored at Sewell's Point and the lights shining over the waters from their portholes. It was the next night (Monday) that the pungy[8] of Capt. John Kendell brought over the 12-pound brass piece from the Navy yard passed the war vessels.

[Some] people said Commodore [J. Garrett] Pendergrast, the U.S. Navy officer in command, was a traitor to his state being a Virginian. Dr. J. Pendergrast Hope, his relative, stood by and said his relative was an old naval officer and was in the Navy many years and did not want to give up his position as he would soon retire and his wife was a northern woman—[these] were his reasons for remaining in the Yankee navy.

The people began to look around for some safe place to move as we were near Fort Monroe and they could shell the town. Many people concluded to leave town until the trouble blew over. The stores had a good stock of goods and very little was moved away as they thought the trouble would be settled and the house goods and furniture would be safe locked up. One boy told his brother to wind up the eight-day clock if he did not get back in time. The people scattered partly at this time to Yorktown, Williamsburg, Norfolk, Portsmouth, and Richmond, but the entire evacuation did not take place until late in May.

The pilots, being state warrant officers, had been ordered not to pilot U.S. vessels and offered their services to Gov. John

8. A smaller form of schooner developed in the 1840s on the Chesapeake Bay to dredge oysters and carry bulk cargo; the name is believed to come from Pungoteague on Virginia's Eastern Shore.

Letcher, although they were nearly all Union men. They took their property (boats) from Hampton to Norfolk or [up] the James River.

The pilot boat *Plume* [owned by Robert C. Wood and others unidentified] was loaded with moveable furniture such as beds, carpets, chairs, crockery, stoves, cooking utensils, bedsteads, safes, etc. The families of Robert Wood, Richard Bully, and Joseph Wingfield were on board [April 22, 1861] waiting for next morning to start up the James River. The war talk was strong on all sides of the water. Steamboats had stopped running. Two Massachusetts regiments had arrived at Old Point.

That night everything was on board and a gay company of friends came on board to bid us goodbye. The moon shone beautiful and all was gay as though off for a frolic, but one of our number had a dark foreboding of the coming storm of war and sat on the windlass forward and wept.

The scene was beautiful in meaning. The boat lay near Hall's [marine] Railway and looking east lay the old Hampton [Queen Street] Bridge where so many pretty girls had promenaded, to the west to Banks [Hotel] and Burcher's Hotel, where summertime dances were held every night.[9]

We slept on the boat that night, some aft and some in the forward bunks. I remember two cockroaches falling in my face waking me up with a start.

We got underway next morning—as the sailor would say, weighed anchor—hoisted the jib and beat out of the creek, where the vessel was never to be entered again by several of the people [on board].

9. The *Plume* lay in the Hampton River at the wharf at the foot of King Street. A physician, Dr. Richard G. Banks, owned and operated the Chesapeake Hotel, which could accommodate 200 guests and had a ballroom, bowling alley, and billiard room, and was situated near the waterfront on Banks Lane. James Burcher operated Kecoughtan Hotel, a smaller hostelry.

When off the Hampton Bar a Yankee schooner hove to for inspection. According to the law, vessels bound north had to be searched for runaway slaves and pay $5 for the search. We bade the schooner to go on.[10] We reached Jamestown that afternoon and fastened to the wharf while a thunderstorm passed over.

I will mention some of the places we passed in getting to Jamestown. We passed the Warwick River, Pagan or Smithfield Creek, Mulberry Island, where the Confederates afterward had a battery [Fort Crawford]. Just across the river a little higher up was Harden's Bluff where they had another battery [Fort Huger]. Grove Wharf was the next lowest point where the regular steamer ran for the first year of the war. Next was Kingsmill, College Creek and Spratley's until we reached Jamestown with Hog Island just across from College Creek.

Next morning we examined the old church ruins and looked over the island. It was owned by Mr. William Allen and Mr. [Gibson] Blake was the overseer. Mr. Armory of Williamsburg was to arrive and meet us and take two of our passengers, Misses Harriet and Josephine Wingfield, to Williamsburg.

Captain Bully and family left in the steamer *Glen Cove* for City Point. When the tide was flood we got underway and sailed up the river—passed across the Chickahominy River, then Sandy

10. The 1860 *Code of Virginia* appointed all harbor pilots as "inspectors" to search "all vessels about to sail or steam from any port or place in this state for any port or place north of and beyond the capes of Virginia . . . to see that no slave, or person held to service or labor in this state, or person charged with the commission of any crime within the state, shall be concealed on board said vessel." Should a slave be found, the pilot "shall attach said vessel, and arrest all persons on board, to be delivered up to the sergeant or sheriff of the nearest port in this commonwealth, to be dealt with according to law." If a runaway slave were found, the pilot was entitled to a $100 reward. The pilot was to be paid a $5 fee for the inspection. If he failed to make an inspection he could be fined $25.

Point, Dillard's Wharf, and anchored at Claremont. Our people had lived near Claremont six years before. We went ashore and visited some of our childhood scenes. We found the place much improved, but the old house where we lived was used as a fodder house.

Claremont is situated at a high point on the river and there were numerous wood shoots along the river bank where the wood was shot down the river banks and loaded on Northern vessels. Looking east from Claremont we see the eastern house of the Seldons, north [across the river] was Sandy Point, west was Lower Brandon, the [ancestral] home of the Harrisons. This place [Claremont] was owned by William Allen.

They had a railroad running through two plantations. We were walking along a trestle about a mile long when we heard the rattle of a snake. We attempted to retreat and heard the locomotive behind. The bottom was a swamp so we advanced slowly and the snake went down the timbers to the swamp. We were frightened to death.

Mr. Allen had everything comfortable at the farm or plantation. Hot houses were foreign to us, beautiful grounds and a long line of quarters for colored people. He owned about 1,100 of these people. He often asked one of the boys, "Who do you belong to?" The boy would say, "You, sir." He would get off his horse and catch hold of a cradle [scythe] and show the darkey how to cut wheat.

A story is told that he was so easy with the people that they got so unruly that he got an old Yankee sailor on the farm. The old overseer called them up and said in his speech: "Niger, Niger, I'se come for to rule dis nation," and began whipping all around, whether they deserved it or not, and frightened them so bad that one of the best hands fell from the loft and was killed, and they sent the overseer away.

Mr. Allen became a major of heavy artillery [Brandon Battery] during the war. Claremont at the present time, 1905, is a thriving town.[11]

In the afternoon [we] sailed up the James, passing Lower and Upper Brandon; Fort Powhatan, where Lafayette [in 1781] is supposed to have crossed in pursuit of Cornwallis; Weyanoke, the home of the Douthats and the scene of Mrs. [Mary] Johnston's story *To Have and to Hold;* Flowerdew, one the earliest settlements on the James; Wilcox Wharf, home of Dr. [Edward] Wilcox; Westover, the red brick mansion erected by Col. William Byrd; Beechwood, Edmund Ruffin's place; Berkeley or Harrison Landing, Jordan's Point, Tar Bay [and] on to City Point where we anchored in the stream in front of the wharfs about 4 o'clock while outlasting a rainy spell that had overtaken us.

City Point was a beautifully situated point made by the James and Appomattox rivers and was a good shipping place at that time, and was General [U. S.] Grant's headquarters in 1864. The depot and wharfs lined the riverfront, and sheds and storehouses were on the wharfs. The track of the branch of the Southside Railroad ran along the riverfront. Great quantities of leaf and other tobacco were shipped from the Point.

Vessels could go to Richmond and take on a load, sinking the

11. George Wood returned to Claremont in the summer of 1906, and reported to the *Richmond Times-Dispatch* that "the old home and kitchen now in a tumble-down state. . . . The old well is still there, about seventy-five feet deep and the water is just as icy. . . . The stump of the old cherry tree at the foot of the lane is standing. The old barn or stable that I used to keep my large gray mule in was torn down. . . . This gray mule, called Champion, I rode to water every day. My brother, who was a large, fat boy, was envious of my horsemanship so he got behind the cherry tree and threw a clod of dirt in the ear of the mule, which caused him to run away, nearly causing my death. On the hill north of town we gathered the bluebottle flowers and in the valley and under the hill, after a rain and north wind, we gathered icicles, sometimes as late as May."

ship up to [a draft of] twelve feet, then sail across the Warwick Bar, drop to City Point and from barges [coming] down the Appomattox and James and the railroad, load to sixteen feet, then cross Harrison's Bar, take on another two feet or more. This to load on at Goose Hill Flats [and] below Jamestown, take on to twenty feet and be ready for sea. Vessels in the foreign trade, such as flour to South America, tobacco to Germany, would often go to Richmond.

At the Gallego Mills and Haxall Mills [canal] turn basin, flour would be rolled out of a barn and [on to barges that would] drop down to the ship locks and [the flour] put in foreign vessels. The James Curry family owned several packets that ran to Rio de Janeiro and that way they saved an immense lot of wagon work.

Some of the barges had a square stern and sharp head and would hold fifty hogsheads of tobacco of a thousand pounds each. She could be put stern on the wharf and tobacco rolled and parbuckled in on the immense timbers that ran lengthwise down her hold.

A large spring was at the bottom of the hill [at City Point] with a stream gushing out that would supply an army with water. On top of the hill were the residences of the people, about twelve or fifteen in number at the first of May when those Hampton people arrived. The inhabitants consisted of Dr. [Richard] Eppes, [who owned Appomattox Manor] where General Grant [later] had his headquarters [June 15, 1864–March 29, 1865], Mr. Procter, stevedore, and Captain Cook, his assistant; Mrs. [Charlotte] Penny, a large 350-pound English woman [who] kept a boarding house or inn; a widow named Mrs. Wood; John Matthews, clerk of Prince George County [who] kept a hotel; Mr. [Jno.] Morris, [who] kept a general store. Joe Cook was telegraph operator; Williams, watchman; Tyler and Collins, fishermen; Banks, ship carpenter; Archer Drew, grocery and post office in Morris' general store. In a few months all closed up on account of the war except Morris, who was a Polish Jew and did considerable trading with the colored people.

We rented a large brick house overlooking the river that had been occupied by a Dr. [C. H.] Tabb, who went off in the army and left a good many residences, and a copy of Dr. [Benjamin] Rush's (the Philadelphia physician), a book that came in very well the next year.[12] The view from this high building—looking east we could see Jordan's Point, Harrison's Landing, Berkeley, and Westover in the distance; north, Bermuda Hundred and Shirley; west looked up the Appomattox River, Cawsons, Broadway, and Port Walthall.

There was a Yankee ship belonging in Boston unloading salt. The captain wanted to get away before the blockade was put on and the men made things merry with their songs while unloading with the tune of:

A Yankee ship and Yankee crew,
Hi-oh, my Johnny.
The captain is a Yankee, too.
Hi-oh, my Johnny.

On this ship a Negro sailor cut the mate badly with a knife, and the people wanted to lynch him. The vessel was towed down the river before the blockade was put on.

The place was a beautiful quiet retreat with [rail] cars running to Petersburg daily. The boys sometime would fish, gather fruit or pick strawberries, hunt terrapin eggs in the sandy beach. It amused them to see many boat loads of colored people coming from Shirley (Hill Carter's plantation), Eppes Island, and Bermuda Hundred with their chickens and eggs on Sunday

12. Here Wood refers to an edition of Benjamin Rush's four-volume *Medical Inquiries and Observations,* published in Philadelphia, first in 1805 and then again in 1809.

morning to exchange for groceries—and coffee, dram,[13] calicoes, and other extras—at Mr. Morris' store.

We thought our Hampton boys were hard nuts, but City Point beat us in the person of Elisha Jenkins. Elisha was about sixteen years old, red-headed and speckled face, and could out cuss anything on two feet, with plenty of horse sense, but did not know a letter as big as your foot. One of our girls gave her eighteenth birthday party and invited Elisha. He arrived "dressed in style" barefooted with pants rolled up to the knees, linen duster to the knees, black beaver hat, white shirt [with a] high standing collar with red tie, and [carrying] a cane.

Old Aunt Eliza Atkins (colored) lived in a small house on the side of the hill and one day the old woman was boiling the pot at her fireplace with a piece of her salt hot greens in the pot. Elisha went to the top of the hill, took an old railroad oil jug and threw it from the top of the hill down her chimney, knocking away the pot, broke the oil jug, scattering water [and] fire all over the floor. The old woman's scream could be heard all over the village and they thought the Yankees were coming. It was Elisha's doings, but could not be proven as he hid in the hill.[14]

13. Whiskey.

14. In another telling of this story, Wood attributes this mischief to Tom Jinks who, along with Tom Wilmot, were "two scamps . . . up to all kinds of dirty work." He says the two Toms were "boon companions" to Billy, who "was no saint himself." In this version "Billy" appears to be a pseudonym for George Wood himself. His embellished account continues:

> Billy, seeing a garden gate open and a large bed of strawberries went in and was stuffing himself when an old Negro woman as black as his satanic majesty rushed at him with a broom handle, saying, "Get out of dare, you." Billy made himself scarce around there. . . .
>
> Tom Wilmot played a prank on the watermelon man by pulling a bunch from out of the cart while he was driving up the hill. An old colored woman would send her 6-year-old boy down the hill to the spring to get a pail of water. He was covered only with a cotton shirt or

We attended the steamers morning and afternoon to hear all the news of the war. There were four steamers running on the river as far [downstream] as Grove Wharf, which is about seven miles from Williamsburg. The Federal frigates *Congress* and *Cumberland* closed or blockaded the James River at Newport News. The steamers were the *Glen Cove,* Captain Davis; *Curtis Peck,* Captain Barnes; *Shultz,* Captain Darius Hill (who ran to Windsor Shade on the Chickahominy River); and *Northampton,* Captain James Hicks.[15] This latter steamer was owned by Captain Hicks, who had used her previously on the Mathews and Eastern Shore route. The Confederate government bought this steamer and ran her for the army. The *Glen Cove, Northampton,* and *Curtis Peck* were sunk in the 1862 obstruction [of the James River] at Fort Darling.

We got [news]papers every morning by these steamers besides from the train from Petersburg and crowds would gather to hear the news and meet many of our people—fugitives fleeing from the Lower Peninsula—going to some point of refuge.

The Old Dominion steamers *Yorktown* and *Jamestown* were in Richmond when the blockade [of the James River] was put on, and they were confiscated by the Southerners and fitted up as men of war. The *Yorktown* was rechristened *Patrick Henry* and the *Jamestown* was called *Thomas Jefferson.* These ships laid out at City Point and took on big guns that were brought on [railroad] flats from the Norfolk navy yard. The *Patrick Henry* had six guns, two on each side and one large gun forward and aft, and was commanded by Capt. [John Randolph] Tucker. The *Thomas Jefferson* had two large guns and was commanded by Lt.

---

gown. Tom called the boy to him and pulled up his shirt and painted him red and sent him home bellowing.

15. James Hicks was George Wood's uncle, his mother's brother. Another brother, William Hicks, owned a wharf in Mathews County.

Cmdr. [Joseph N.] Barney. They also had a man-of-war tug, *Teaser,* commanded by Lieutenant Webster. These boats cruised no further than Day's Point [Fort Boykin] and lay most of the time at Mulberry Island. Some days they would run down near enough to fire a shot at the blockading ships, *Congress* and *Cumberland,* anchored at Newport News, and return.

In a few weeks we were joined by Captains [James] Minson, [Charles] Topping, [William] Clark, [James] Massenburg, [William] Curtis, and [James] Turner.

Of our family there were Sam, George (myself), Ned, Matt [Martha] (still single), Emma, Keturah (Mrs. Pope), Elizabeth (Mrs. Wingfield). William came up with the Massenburg family.[16] J[ohn] B. remained at Yorktown and ran tugs. R[obert] B. was a Union man and was held in Confederate prison.

The Hampton family remained idle [at City Point] for several months.[17]

Federal Soldiers Enter Hampton

"Ready and Spoiling for a Fight"

In Hampton, as soon as Virginians ratified the Ordinance of Succession, young men, many of them students at Cary's Military Academy,

16. William Wood was "disabled at Yorktown handling a mortar" and came to City Point with his in-laws.

17. In an undated newspaper clipping found in his journal, George Wood recalls a fish fry held at City Point to celebrate Independence Day 1861. "We [the refugees from Hampton], of course, naturally expected these gentlemen [of Prince George County] to enjoy the sport of catching the fish, but instead they brought their colored men along to haul the seines, while they sat under the trees on the banks of the Appomattox [River] . . . playing cards and regaling themselves with iced mint julep, etc. This was the first time I ever saw a Confederate shinplaster (25-cent note) and the last time I saw 25-cent silver pieces in the Confederacy."

rushed to enlist in the Wythe Rifles, which became Company A of the Thirty-second Virginia Infantry Regiment; the Hampton Grays, which became Company E of that regiment; and the Old Dominion Dragoons, which became Company B of the Third Virginia Cavalry.

In a rapid sequence of events, Confederate troops confronted Union soldiers probing Hampton from Fort Monroe, but no shots were fired. Citizens—several with conflicted loyalties—left their homes.

Nothing of importance transpired [in Hampton] until about the 10th or 15th of May. The Federals had at this time three regiments at Fort Monroe and [fresh] water was scarce, and besides [they] wanted more room for encampment, and they marched over Mill Creek Bridge, the Southern picket falling back to Colonel [Thomas] Tabb's place. The Federals took possession of Captain Clark's place at the bridge on the waterfront and encamped there.

When the Southern pickets had to leave their post, they returned to Hampton with the news that the Yankees were coming. The people turned out in a mass and rushed to the [Queen Street] bridge [over the Hampton River] as Col. [Robert H.] Armistead of Williamsburg said to repel the invader. The jingle of swords could be heard all along the pavements. The two 6-pound guns and 12-pound brass piece were full with powder and mounted at Mr. H. L. Schmelz's place [which was at the western side of the Queen Street Bridge in 1905]. Old men and boys were there with double-barrel guns loaded with buckshot and ready for a round, but the Federals came no further. If they had come to Hampton on that day, Hampton would have been the Lexington of the Civil War as the people were ready and spoiling for a fight. The Confederate picket line was then established at east side of Hampton Bridge.

Lt. William R. Vaughan of the Old Dominion Dragoons, who

"Fort Monroe, Virginia," from the *Illustrated London News,* May 25, 1861, p. 499. (Special Collections, University of Virginia)

was officer of the day, rode down to the fort under a flag of truce and demanded of Col. Justin Dimick, commander of the fort, "By what right, sir, do you invade this sacred soil of Virginia?" The old colonel replied, "By God, sir, might makes right."

On the fourth Thursday in May [the 23rd] was the spring election day, and the Ordinance of Secession was to be submitted to the [ratification] vote of the people, and there were several Union men in town. Among them was the Hon. Joseph Segar, who stuck by the Union to the last. There was also Mr. K[ennon] Whiting and R[obert] B. Wood.

Three of Col. [Charles King] Mallory's slaves—Jim Townsend, Isaac Monroe, and Frank Baker—had gone to Old Point to gain their freedom. Major [George] Wray [of the 115th Virginia Militia], agent for Colonel Mallory, and Col. J. B. Cary went to Old

"The Contraband of War," showing Militia Major John Baytop Cary conferring while on horseback with General Benjamin Butler at the bridge over Mill Creek outside Fort Monroe. (From Benjamin F. Butler, *Butler's Book: Autobiography and Personal Reminiscences,* Boston: A. M. Thayer & Co., 1892)

Point to get their recovery, and there General Butler treated them very courteously but refused to give them up and treated the slaves as contrabands of war, hence the name applied to colored people as contrabands. Butler made use of them on fortifications and other government work.

Col. [J. Wolcott] Phelps of 1st Vermont regiment marched up to Hampton. Some boys had set fire to the bridge. Colonel Phelps called out through a trumpet, "Put out that fire," and several people put the fire out. A few buckets of water stopped the conflagration. The regiment marched to the Cross Streets [the intersection of King and Queen streets], halted for a few minutes and returned to the other side of Hampton Bridge. Not more then half dozen people were visible; all had left town.

The soldiers heard of the proposed [Federal] occupation of Newport News [Point] by water and were afraid of being cut off by the New Market Road and therefore retreated by the Back River Road.

On the 27th the Confederates decided to evacuate Hampton for Yorktown leaving all their possessions behind them as General Butler had occupied Newport News with Colonel Phelps' 1st Vermont Regiment, and the Hampton forces could be cut off at any time. People scattered to all parts of the state—Richmond, Norfolk, Petersburg—and North Carolina. Major Hope gives a lively description of our people on the retreat gathering at the different places in the route under shade trees, resting and eating as though on a picnic.

Our people, though, had access to the town as no Federals were on the west side of Hampton [River]. Our soldiers would come in by way of New Market [Road] and go out the new [Back River Road] bridge way.

Mr. F. A. Schmelz, one of our old citizens and merchant, went with the troops to Yorktown. Mr. Schmelz was born in Germany, came as a soldier at Fort Monroe about 1832. He was a baker by profession and was at once detached as a baker. When his time was up, he came to Hampton (1838), bought Dr. Colton's place, corner of Queen and Wine streets. He carried his cakes, bread, and pies around in baskets and carts, and, as was predicted by some, became the wealthiest man in our town. He baked for the Southern men at Yorktown and moved with the troops to Richmond and made money and invested the Confederate money in property. He returned after the war, continued in business, increased his wealth and died in 1881. He was a good example for many of our boys to follow.

One of our industrious and prosperous farmers, John Armistead, went to Richmond. The old gentleman did not know what to do and got a job at the shipyard.

He told his son, Sam, "I got a job."

51

a Cold dark rainey night May 3rd arrived [illegible]
Richmond about day light. When the evac
took place our company were Stationed a[s]
follows - Wythe Rifles at Yorktown and Wa[rwick]
Morters. Grays at Camp Page just out side
Wmburg. The Dagroons Were doing Vedette
and Scouting all over the pennunsular [illegible]
used as guides and their Servises Were [illegible]
The Washington art Was at Ship point [illegible]
Point made by Chisman's Creek and the
River. One night the Summer of 1861 a p[icket]
fired at A Star rising thought it [was]
a yankee gun boat Coming up the
river and roused the Whole Comma[nd]
he was one of the up County Soldiers Who [had]
never seen a boat - There Was Seven
Malitia Companies Who had not been [in]
in a Volenteer Companies one Commanded by
Brown on by Capt Hogg, they Were as[signed]
to Companies after the avacuation and the[y]
found other peaces - Many of our Men returned
after the avacuation especialy those Who Were
sick to the War. Many of our people Who w[ished]
to remain nutral who had union Sentiments a[nd]
did not Want to do anything aganst their Sta[te]
friends or help the U S forces Were not allowed
by neutral by the Southern men and Were
Carried to yorktown and Some of them returned
after the evacuation. R. B. Wood one of the union
men Was Captured in august 1861 at the hom[e]

"What is it, Father?"

"Turning the grindstone, Sonny."

He got a place as overseer on a farm at Bonsack. His son told him to get a ticket at the depot. He went off repeating "Bonsack." A horse ran away, and [in the excitement] he forgot the name, and the [depot] agent asked him to stand [away] from the [ticket] window until he could remember the station. A young lady came to the window and asked for her ticket to Bonsack. The old man threw his arms around her and said, "God bless you. I have been trying to remember that name." It frightened the lady for a moment, but he soon made her acquainted with the situation.

Many of our men returned home after the evacuation, especially those who were opposed to the war. Many of our people who wished to remain neutral or who had Union sentiments and did not want to do anything against their state, or friends, or help the U.S. forces, were not allowed to be neutral by the Southern men and were carried to Yorktown, and some of them returned after the evacuation.

John ["Captain Jack"] Young was an illiterate man, but of good memory and when a man asked him how he made out [during the Civil War], he said: "I had a very bad time. I could not go in the woods to get wood for fires. The marauders (guerillas) would get after me. Could not go fishing for fear the torpedoes would blow you up, or buy a barrel of flour without getting a permit."

The old man said when the Yankees first came to Hampton [one could see] the glitter of the guns of the 1st Vermont Regiment, Colonel Phelps, coming around Tabb's Corner [on the east side of the Queens Street bridge]. Bill Howell, who lived in Pee Dee, was looking across the mist from the Academy yard. Bill rushed down the road to the water and passing the house cried out, "Come on, Mary Ann (wife), or the damn Yankees will get us," and rushing in the mud and water began to push his boat on in the river. Looking back and in his squeaky voice he said, "Hurry up, Mary Ann, or the damn Yankees will get us." She finally appeared on the shore with her bundle and he took her in his arms, waded out to the boat, put her in and laid his course up the head of the creek.

The soldiers went back in an hour to the fort.

When Captain Jack was taken before General [John E.] Wool, charged with harboring Southern soldiers, the general, after questioning him, said, "Mr. Young, I am very sorry to have to send you to the Rip Raps Prison."

"Well, general, if you feel sorry, how do you think I feel?"

He was released.

Fighting at Big Bethel and the Burning of Hampton

"No Houses to Live In"

While not a witness to the Wythe Rifles dashing to battle at Big Bethel Church or the Federals' humiliating return to Fort Monroe, George Wood offered a partisan Southern account of the June 10, 1861, fight into which both sides blundered.

Nor was Wood present on the night of August 7 when Confederate troops—including several local men—deliberately set fire to homes, businesses, and churches in Hampton. He rationalized that the conflagration was ordered to prevent contrabands from occupying vacated homes, a fear based on an unsubstantiated story in a Northern newspaper.

Wood relied on two published accounts to support his justification of the burning: "To Disabuse the Northern Mind" by Captain S. W. Armistead in the April 1875 issue of the *Southern Worker*, and an anony-

mous article in the August 7, 1911, *Boston Globe,* "To Prevent the Possible Concentration of Contraband Negroes by Gen. Butler."

Much of his understanding of these critical events came from anecdotal stories told by participants well after the war. And no doubt he had help compiling lists of evacuees, of men who served in the military, and of buildings destroyed.

The Wythe Rifles were engaged in the [June 10, 1861] Battle of Bethel, nine miles from Hampton, the first battle of the war. The Rifles and Old Dominion Dragoons were the only troops engaged from Hampton. The Rifles were commanded by Lt. Samuel R. Chisman, and during the charge, Charles Henry Collier, a member, gave the first Rebel Yell that the Yankees talked so much about afterwards.

The Federals came up from Old Point to Hampton [and] crossed over a pontoon bridge. They were New York and Massachusetts regiments with a regular battery of artillery. The artillery was under Lt. John T. Grebel, who was killed. Grebel Lodge of Odd Fellows is named after him.

Brig. Gen. [Ebenezer W.] Pierce, who had his headquarters at a residence opposite Barnes Hotel, commanded the expedition. They started for Bethel on the early morning of June 10, and when they arrived at New Market met a regiment from Newport News who in the fog did not know them, [and] fired on their own men, killing and wounding about twenty-five.

The Rifles were several miles away and double quicked to the battlefield to commence the fight. Gen. Bankhead Magruder was in command of the Southern troops composed of the 1st North Carolina Regiment; Wythe Rifles; J. Thompson Brown's Artillery (Richmond); Charles City troops, Captain [Robert] Douthat; Old Dominion Dragoons, Capt. J. C. Phillips. While the fight was going on, a church hid the Yankees who sheltered themselves behind it, and volunteers were called to burn the church. Three men of the North Carolina regiment volunteered and set fire to the church. They were returning when young [Private Henry L.] Wyatt [of North Carolina] was mortally wounded—the first to be killed, his head shot off by a cannon ball. A [Confederate] battery was unsupported and the New York regiment Zouaves charged to take it. The Wythe Rifles charged from one direction and the North Carolina regiment from another when Charles Henry Collier gave the Rebel Yell. When they arrived near the battery the North Carolina regiment pounded in a volley and the Zouaves broke and ran. This ended the battle.

Captain Phillips wanted to follow up and capture the enemy's cannon, but was refused permission to advance. There were many dead left on the field. Lieutenant Grebel was taken back on a caisson, and all the conveyances around the neighborhood were used to take the wounded back. About fifty to seventy-five were killed and wounded.

Maj. [Theodore] Winthrop, 5th New York [aide to General Butler], and several others were buried in one grave, but next day a flag of truce came up and [the officer in charge] asked for his body, which was dug up and sent to Old Point, where it was sent North to his friends.

General Butler reprimanded General Pierce for failure in the expedition saying General Pierce was absent-minded, and Pierce retorted that if he were absent-minded Butler was absent in body. The Confederates could have been easily flanked, and when the Federals withdrew from the fight they thought it was for the purpose of a flank movement.

General Magruder said, "God never made a better day for men to die," and the remark was not altogether cheering to new recruits. Bill Hope of the Wythe Rifles replied that it didn't make any difference to him what kind of a day it was if he had to die.

Most of the Yankees never shot a gun before, and all the leaves of the trees were cut off; the balls went over the heads of the Southern men. The Federals lost in killed and wounded sixty men, and they retreated.

The Confederates lost two or three wounded; one [Private Henry L.] Wyatt of the North Carolina regiment died. These wounded men got their wounds in a volunteer expedition across the farm to burn the church that hid the enemy. A monument was erected to their memory in 1905.

Lieutenant [Samuel R.] Chisman commanded the Wythe Rifles and was complimented by the commanding officers. He was promoted a major in the Quartermaster Department where he served the balance of the war. He died about 1885.

On the retreat, part of the [Federal] forces returned through Hampton and a part to Newport News. Those going over to Camp Hamilton (U.S. camp [now Phoebus]) went over [the Hampton River] in boats as the bridge burnt the last of May. The bridge was rebuilt about the first of July 1861. The Union forces raised the U.S. flag on Hampton on July 4.

The Daughters of the Confederacy has given Mrs. [Hannah Nicholson] Tunnell great credit for warning the Southern troops of the Yankees' approach, but she must have warned the scouting party on the left wing over on the Back River Road and prevented them from being cut off from the Bethel line. Mr. Lyn Etheridge of the Old Dominion Dragoons, one of the pickets, certainly gave the alarm of their approach. The Dragoons were the only one of our company active at the front doing courier work.

The day before this battle the North Carolina regiment had a skirmish on the Back River Road with the Federals, and the morning of the advance Mr. A. L. Whiting was captured and his father's house (Henry Whiting's) was burnt by the Federals on Back River.

Our men were armed mostly with smooth-bore muskets that were loaded in the muzzle with powder, a ball, and three buckshots. John Rodgers, a big Eastern Shoreman who was a blacksmith in Hampton, wanted to be put two hundred yards in the rear as his gun scattered so [that this way] he could kill more of the Yankees. The fact was he was frightened.

On the 7th of August General Magruder determined to burn Hampton to prevent the Yankees and Negroes from occupying the houses. Messages were sent to warn the people to get out of town. These messengers were mostly members of the Old Dominion Dragoons.

There were about ten or twelve white families living in the town and many colored people. Among the whites were Col. Wilson Jones, Cary Wood, William House, J. D. Hosier, John D. Hicks, John Langley, Mrs. Green and Mrs. Smith, Diana Robinson, Jack Hicks.[18]

General Magruder came with a large force to New Market to protect the firing party from the Federals at Newport News and sent Major [James G.] Hodges [of the Fourteenth Virginia Regiment]; Old Dominion Dragoons, Captain [Jefferson C.] Phillips; Charles City Troop, Captain [Robert] Douthart; York Rangers, Captain [Jefferson] Sinclair, to do the firing. Each road was picketed and men marched through to the [Queen Street] bridge. The Federals were over at Colonel Tabb's place and Colonel Mallory's place (now G. A. Schmelz's) and fired on them [and they] also pulled up the plank of the bridge and made a barricade. Several shots were fired, which did not harm the South side; one ball entered the blanket of a man.

The firing of the buildings was commenced on each side of Queen Street and the wind being east[ward] they started west

18. The relationship, if any, of Cary Wood to George R. Wood is unstated and unknown.

as they fired. Several houses in Pee Dee were not burnt but pulled down afterwards by a Maine regiment. Many of the men set fire to their own houses. Mr. W. Jones was sick and had to be taken out to Mr. Fayette Sinclair's place.

James Scofield, a northern Union man, who was boarding at Captain Kenner's above the Baptist Church and kept his [beer and tobacco] store at Joe Phillips' livery stable (about at Ransome Bros.' Store), was sent for, and he opened his store for the boys to get what they wanted. The men liked him though he was a Yankee. He was taken as far as Mr. Fayette Sinclair's when he was released. (He was killed about ten years after the war on the Eastern Shore, Maryland, by a Negro robber who broke into his store.)

A very good account of the burning of Hampton was written by Capt. S. W. Armistead after the war and published in the *Southern Worker.*

Mr. J. C. King says the Fifteenth Virginia Regiment was down in Hampton on the 7th and warned people to leave. He says an article in the *New York Herald* from Fort Monroe advising the U.S. Government to quarter the Negro contraband in the vacant houses caused General Magruder to consent to the burning of Hampton. He says Dr. Samuel Shield gave him the paper with the article in it but did not know about the article at the time and that Magruder, being drunk at the time, gave the order. Colonel Cary, Major Wray, Dr. Vaughan, and Robert Vaughan had persuaded him to burn it before, but he had refused. Dr. Shield was sorry after reading the article that he had given the paper to General Magruder.

Sergeant [John T.] Howard of the York Rangers, one of our Hampton boys, says the drug stores of S. R. Chisman and F. Massenburg & Cary made a big fire with the large amount of paint, oil, varnish, and burning fluid (used in those days in lamps for light). He set fire to Mrs. Watts' building opposite

Barnes Hotel and under a fine piano, which played as the fire warmed up. Also Parker West's immense wooden store and dwelling at the corner of Queen and Hope streets.

They told Cary Wood to get out as they were going to burn the house down. He quietly blackened his shoes. He is said to have had a clean start.[19]

19. George Wood compiled a random running list of public buildings, business establishments, and residences destroyed in the fire of August 7, 1861. He apparently added to the list from time to time, and here and there his handwriting is illegible. He misspelled some names and made what may be a few redundant entries. His list, which follows, has been checked against the census for 1860 and, whenever possible, verified, and confirmations made accordingly.

2 brick Methodist Episcopal churches on Wine Street; 1 brick mill on Brown Street; 1 brick Methodist Episcopal Church on Queen Street (partly perished); 1 brick MP Church on Queen Street; 1 brick Baptist Church on King Street; Brick courthouse; St. John's [Episcopal Church] (walls saved).

K[ennon] Whiting at wharf 2 brick houses (walls saved); Mrs. Eliza Face, brick residence on head of Locust Street; H. M. Jones, brick residence on Locust and Cary Streets; Mrs. [Laura] Garrett, brick residence, Queen Street; William Anderson, brick residence, Queen Street; Dr. G[eorge] W. Semple, brick residence, Queen Street.

Mrs. Eliza Face, brick store rooms above; Samuel Cummings, 2 brick stores residence above; Thomas D. Peek; Capt. Brown, brick stores below, residence above.

Gill A. Cary, store; Mr. [Robert A.] Armistead's brick residence one end, store at other; F. H. Schmelz, 2 brick stores, residence above; S[amuel] R. Chesman store on Queen Street.

Property of Dr. [William R.] Vaughan, all on Queen Street; Jeff Sinclair, store below office above, King Street; Mrs. [Ann] Goodwin; Mr. [Hercules] Savage; Mrs. Eliza Jones; Kecoughtan House, [James] Burcher['s] Hotel; William Jennings; Fayette Jones; Col. Wilson Jones.

Thomas Watts, King Street business; R. E. Bennet, grocer, Locust Street; W. L. Westwood, Wine and Queen, grocer; Seabury Shoe Store; Samuel Cummings, Queen Street, millinery and dry goods; [Columbus] Jett and Wray, wood store, dry goods; William Face, [illegible].

M[arion] Colbert, books; S. R. Chisman, dry goods and hardware; [William] Massenburg & Cary, dry goods and hardware; Post Office; F. A.

Many of the incidents would be told from one to the other as we meet at different places where the people were located. No one cared to go back to Hampton as there were no houses to live in.

On August 7, 1861, all went up in smoke: five brick churches and another not brick, twenty-eight brick residences, twenty-six business places, [and] a large number of handsome wooden dwellings.

The following are some of the people and places where they went:

Mrs. Eliza Jones and daughter to North Carolina.

W. S. Jones family to Petersburg.

Dr. Semple to Richmond. He was a surgeon.

Dr. Hope to Richmond. He was a surgeon.

Captains Tom and Jim Cunningham family to Richmond, in river transportation Quartermaster Department.

M. Colbert family to Richmond. Boat Building in transportation Quartermaster Department.

John A. Curtis to Richmond, Quartermaster Department and Navy.

Frank Guy to Richmond, Quartermaster Department.

Schmelz, grocery and baker; Pasco H. Latimer, grocery and liquor; N[athaniel] Gammel, grocer; W. W. Darden [taylor]; M[artha] Taylor; A[dolphe] Adler, clothier; J. D. Peek & Son, dry goods.

C[yrus H.] Wineburger, baker; Mrs. [Elizabeth] Divine, millinery; Mrs. Cooper, millinery; Mrs. [Mary] Lake, dry goods; Mrs. [Judith] Stores, dry goods; [illegible]; James Scofield, liquor, beer saloon, King Street; T[homas] V. Moss, jeweler, Queen Street.

Kit K[illegible], stationery, Queen Street; [William] Samuel Tompkins, grocer; H[enry] C[lay] Whiting, King Street, grocer and liquor; Thomas Watts, grocery, wooden building; [illegible]; T. W. Roche; Joe Phillips, livery stable.

According to Wood, the assessed value of land and houses in Hampton in 1861 was $242,749, of which $172,450 was in buildings destroyed. In 1892, he wrote, the value of real estate in Hampton was estimated to be about $2,750,000.

George Booker and family to Richmond, Pay Department.

Dr. [William R.] Vaughan, surgeon, to Petersburg.

F[rederick] Palmer to Charlotte, N.C. Machine Shop.

John Gammel to Richmond, Ordnance Department.

John Armistead to Richmond, afterwards Danville. Engineer Department. Died at hospital, Williamsburg.

Charles Topping, R. Bully, J. Minson, J. Turner to Westover.

Robert Wood to City Point, Rowland's Mill, Richmond and Weston.

Lieutenant Colonel J. B. Cary, paymaster.

F. A. Schmelz, Richmond.

Captain H. C. Whiting, Quartermaster Department, Richmond and North Carolina.

Captain J. W. Brown, Richmond and North Carolina, Quartermaster Department.

Capt. James Hicks, C. S. Transportation Service, Richmond.

Capt. Samuel Wood, Transportation Service, Petersburg.

C. Wineburger to Williamsburg.

W. W. Duran to Williamsburg.

John A. Curtis to Quartermaster Department and Navy, Richmond.

Parker West to Richmond.

G. B. West to Richmond, Quartermaster Department.

The following men held other places in the war outside of the regular company that went from here:

Lieutenant Colonel J. B. Cary, Pay Department; Dr. R. G. Banks, surgeon; R. G. Banks of Quartermaster; Captain H. C. Whiting, lieutenant, Lee Guards [and] afterwards on staff as captain and quartermaster; Frank Lee, Lee Guards, Warwick; John Pembroke Jones, captain, C.S.N.; Thomas M. Jones, colonel, infantry; John Simpkins Jones, quartermaster; William Parker, Richmond Howitzers; John Booker, Signal Corps; E. M. Semple, major and assistant adjutant general, General Ewell's staff; Colonel Joe Ham, colonel, 16th Virginia Infantry; Andrew Armistead, captain artillery; L. H. Sclater, Richmond Howitzers; George W. Armistead, master, C.S.N.; G. M. Peek, General O'Neal's staff and afterwards lieutenant and professor of mathematics, C.S.N.; W. D. Rudd, Company E, 61st Regiment; F. W. Jett, major, engineer; John T. Giddings, Dabney's Battery; Charles K. Mallory, colonel, militia; Captain of Militia J. W. Brown, R. L. Hogg, John Thomas, James Watkins. W. R. Jenning, surgeon. James Sclater, quartermaster sergeant. Frank Brittingham (Navy). Henry Joynes, Carter's Battery. R. Nance (Navy). Thomas Cunningham, James Cunningham, Frank Guy, Charles Topping, R[obert C.] Wood, S. B. Wood, George R. Wood, Junius Turner, Quartermaster Transportation Service; G. B. West, Quartermaster Department. Thomas Cunningham, pilot, Navy; Joe Young, pilot, Navy; C. K. Mallory Jr., Navy. Captain James Hicks, Transportation Quartermaster; Captain Thomas Massenburg, Signal Corps. C. J. Ost, Ordnance Department; W. R. Laws, Engineer Department; Dr. W. H. Peek, surgeon. D. W. Mahone, Jeffrys Battery. L. H. Sclater [name crossed out]. George Booker, Richmond Howitzers; J. C. King, 15th Virginia; Captain Jeff Sinclair, Captain W. J. Stores, Lieutenant R. O. Willis (killed), Tom Cane, Tom Forsyth, Elijah Foster, John T. Howard, Tom Herbert, E. K. Peek served in the York Rangers. Major [George] Wray served on Magruder's staff. Lieutenant Joe Phillips, General Magruder's staff. James Massenburg, Quartermaster Department, later substitute artillery died in prison (Delaware).

Frank Lee, Capt., Lee Guards, died in service [at Vicksburg]. W. K. Tabb, Capt., instructor; Capt. [illegible]; Joe Ham, Colonel, 16th Virginia, wounded.

Supplying Confederate Troops

"I Went as a Deckhand"

Confederate authorities appointed Robert C. Wood to command the captured schooner *James Buchanan,* to serve as a receiving ship for unloading military supplies from the steamer *Northampton.* George Wood accompanied his father aboard the *Buchanan* and, for a while, was joined by his brother, Sam. They made stops at wharfs along the James, Chickahominy, and Appomattox rivers, and George swapped stories with friends from Hampton who were camped at Williamsburg.

Capt. Samuel Skinner commanded a large side-wheel steamer named the *William Allison,* which was sometimes used as a transport on the river. Capt. Thomas Cunningham commanded the town's one other side-wheel boat; Capt. Frank Guy, the tug *Seaboard;* and Capt. John Trower, the tug boat *Banner.*

The Confederates had seized the two U.S. schooners, *James Buchanan* and *North Wind* that had been used as a buoy tender and lightboat,[20] and used them for carrying stores from the *Northampton.*

On September 15 [1861] father took command of the transport schooner *James Buchanan* to carry stores for the Confederates and I went as a deckhand or sailor.

We anchored [for a few months] off the mouth of College

20. A vessel (also known as a lightship) whose stationary position is marked on navigational charts and sends out steady or flashing light signals visible by passing navigators to enable them to fix their position—as would a buoy. John W. Vaughan, fifty-three, of Hampton, is identified in the 1860 census as "keeper lightboat."

Creek as a store boat to receive government stores from the steamer *Northampton* at night, put the stores on board a barge [also called a "canal boat" by Wood] and poled or rowed her up the creek to Williamsburg to Captain Hope's commissary.

One afternoon we worked until dark, got off before a storm ran up the creek, but did not get to the landing until daylight. We walked up to Williamsburg and arrived very tired and hungry, went in an eating house and who should we find but old Aunt Mary Ann Massenburg. She had moved up from Hampton when our town was evacuated. She said, "All right, Honey, I will soon have your breakfast." We were famished and enjoyed our ham, eggs, and coffee. She was in the same business in Hampton, and every boy knew her and had eaten her molasses candy. She died about 1890 from being burnt badly while making molasses candy in a place next to Greble Hall.

Our trips to Jamestown [were made] while [the island was] commanded by Capt. Catesby ap Jones, one of the best officers and men, and dealing with him was pleasant. He afterwards was on the *Merrimack* or *Virginia* as executive officer, and when Adm. [Franklin] Buchanan was wounded he took command.

It was while at Jamestown we noticed the good shooting of some of the Brunswick County artillery. Shooting the cattle they butchered they would put a ball from a musket every time in the forehead of the beast.

It was then I first saw a drown man, a Negro from the *Northampton,* floating around. He fell from the Jamestown wharf while loading. We buried him in the sand on the shore.

Richard Bully, mate, and John Treaty, sailor, left us at Jamestown. Their places were supplied by James Grant and S. B. Wood, the latter to act as mate. James Grant took the cook's place.

We sailed the river and got on casks of water from Mulberry Island and shot and shell for the *Patrick Henry,* Captain [John

Randolph] Tucker. At Mulberry Island we saw a barge drifting out of Skiffes Creek, and the man had poles only long enough to shove the barge along the shore with a party of Georgia soldiers aboard. The wind took them off land, and [without paddles or sails] they would have gone to the Yankees down river, but we sailed to them, caught them, then threw a rope and towed them back in safety—and [they] were very thankful.

We carried a load to the *Patrick Henry* [where] George Gifford, son of the celebrated James River steamboat captain, was master's mate. Our intercourse with Captain Tucker of the *Patrick Henry* (*Yorktown*), to whom we carried shot, shell, and coal, was pleasant.

The next trip to Williamsburg I visited the Hampton Grays [Company E, Thirty-second Virginia Regiment] at the College Yard. They used the college [the main building of William and Mary now called the Sir Christopher Wren Building] for a hospital. Jim Davis said he carried bread pills [a placebo] every day to a fellow who said he had rheumatism. The patient said it did him so much good. The boys laughed at him as a coward, and the doctor kept up the joke. Several of the boys, among them Lewis Dobbins [and] Jim Topping, were detailed for work as cowherds[men]. I ate dinner with them and they laughed because I took off my hat at dinner.

While in Williamsburg we saw many Hampton people who were there as refugees and also many of our soldiers. The Washington Artillery was then at Ship's Point, a point made by Chisman Creek and the Poquoson River; Wythe Rifles [Company A, Thirty-second Virginia Regiment] at Yorktown and working mortars; Grays at Camp Page outside Williamsburg; and Old Dominion Dragoons doing picket duty and scouting all over the peninsula.

The artillery had a good time at Ship's Point. One of the upper county men who was doing sentinel duty one night, saw the moon rising out of the water and mistaking its bright red glare for the fires of a Yankee gunboat, fired his gun and alarmed the whole camp.

They tell a yarn on Davis. He went out to buy a gallon of milk. He asked the man for a peck of potatoes 50 cents. He got the man to exchange them for a peck of turnips. Then got him to exchange for a gallon of milk and started off without paying.

The man said, "You owe me 50 cents for the milk."

"No, I don't. I gave you the turnips for the milk."

But the man said, "You did not pay for the turnips."

But he said, "I gave you the potatoes for the turnips."

The farmer got so confused that he said, "Take the milk and go, but I don't sell you anything more."

We carried a load of wood from Rockahock[21] on the Chick-

21. At Rockahock, Robert C. Wood claims ownership of a boat he left in Hampton, a twenty-eight-foot log canoe that a barge captain found abandoned and seized. The story of the *Saucy Jack* is told by George Wood in an undated clipping from an unidentified newspaper that he pasted in one of his journal books.

> I will give a short history of the canoe *Saucy Jack*. The *Saucy Jack* belonged to a Hampton gentleman and was built by David Taylor of York County. She was 28-feet long. The boys of Cary's Academy, and in fact nearly all the boys around, used her for sailing and fishing expeditions, so that she was always in requisition.
>
> In April 1861 the owner left her in Hampton and went up the James River, never expecting to see her again. In February 1862, while loading wood at Rockahock on the Chickahominy in the schooner *James Buchanan* he saw the canoe alongside of a canal barge commanded by Captain Mull. He recognized *Saucy Jack* at once and inquired of Mull where he came across the boat. The captain said the last trip he made up the Warwick River he found her on the shore. (Warwick River was as far [upstream on the James River] as the Southern people dare venture as it was in full sight of the *Cumberland* and *Congress* which lay at the mouth of the James River.)
>
> The captain cheerfully turned the boat over to her rightful owner, who found out afterward how she came to be so far away from home. One of

ahominy River [in New Kent County]. I advanced the river with large cypress trees growing in the water and paddled my boat all around to shoot ducks. I think of John Smith's history when he was captured up this river.

[We carried] two loads of wood from Broadway on the Appomattox, one from Gills Landing, one from Bermuda Hundred. [We carried] two loads of corn from City Point. We made two loads of commissary stores from Petersburg. There we got acquainted with Major Branch, the commissary who married Miss Lowry of Back River.

Late in 1861 we were called to City Point to attend the funeral

---

the Hampton boys was moving his family in her up the James River, but when off Pig Point [on the Southern shore opposite Newport News Point], the *Harriet Lane* was so close that they deemed it wise not to proceed further, so they landed at the point, leaving the boat on the shore. That night a Southern Union man went to Newport News in her and left the boat on the shore. At flood tide the boat drifted away and reached the Warwick River where Captain Mull found her. (The man who crossed to Newport News in her entered the Union navy and was killed in action.)

The boat was taken [in tow] to Richmond and kept in the basin for some time. When the Federal fleet advanced up the James River, the owner of the *Saucy Jack* returned to City Point, leaving the boat behind and never expecting to see her again. I took her to Bermuda Hundred in December 1863 and paddled through the ice to Weston on the Appomattox River to spend four hours with my people on Christmas Day.

When the family left Weston, being within the Union line, they came to Hampton, leaving the boat at the landing. A colored man was seen in the canoe three months afterwards and refused to give her up as he had paid $5 for her. My brother proved the property and took the case to Provost Marshal Major Cassell. He ordered the boat returned without pay and directed the darkey be put in guard house if he complained.

Thus the canoe followed us all through the way and back to Hampton and laid up on the shore of the old homestead for about ten years and finally was sawed in two and made a duck house in 1872.

of Mrs. Jefferson "Joe" Wingfield (sister Elizabeth), who had been sick a long time.

We spent our first Christmas at City Point and it was spoiled by one of the boys taking too much of the old mellow peach brandy that [had] belonged to the Yankees and was confiscated and held there. They [the boys] got the privilege of the depot agent to broach it. We thought as it was [so] sweet and good [that] it would not make drunk come. One [fellow] played violin and the bones and other instruments while singing and making merry Xmas. I knew nothing afterward until next morning.

The Battle of the *Virginia* and the *Monitor*

"Shoe Deep with Blood and Brains"

Throughout their lives, Confederates who fought in the March 1862 Battle of the Ironclads (also known as the Battle of Hampton Roads) were celebrated and revered, and none more than "Hampton's champion fighter" Richard A. Curtis aboard the CSS *Virginia* and Midshipman Charles Mallory aboard the CSS *Beaufort.* Their stories quickly became folklore and the basis for George Wood's what-if wishful thinking about the capture of Fort Monroe and a naval fight off Jamestown Island by the Confederate ironclad that had been scuttled.

As Union General George B. McClellan's Army of the Potomac advanced up the Peninsula, George Wood's schooner evacuated supplies from Kingsmill Wharf and artillerymen from Jamestown to Richmond.

We were too high up the river to see the [March 9, 1862] fight between the *Virginia* and the *Monitor,* but have talked with one who was [a gunner] on board of the *Merrimack,* Richard Curtis. Dick was Hampton's champion fighter, but he got enough that day.

Illustration of the March 9, 1862, Battle of Hampton Roads between the USS *Monitor* and the CSS *Virginia.* (From Joseph A. Joel, *Rifle Shots and Bugle Notes,* New York: Grand Army Gazette Publishing Company, 1884)

Former Governor [William E.] Cameron gives an accurate account of the fight with very little to be added. The *Virginia* made a mistake [on March 8] in running into the [USS] *Cumberland* too hard as it ruined [the *Virginia*'s] prow before she could back out, and the weight of the great ship going down twisted the prow [and] caused her to leak forward. Half the force [would have been] sufficient.

Charles Mallory, midshipman on the [CSS] *Beaufort,* stepped on board of the [USS] *Congress.* The decks were shoe deep with blood and brains, showing she and consort fought well. He was offered the sword of [Lieutenant William Smith,] the commanding officer, which he turned over to his superior officer. Charles was son of Colonel [Charles K.] Mallory and an old academy boy. He was killed down the Mississippi River later in the war.

This attack of the [CSS] *Virginia* was merely a test, and if they could have known her power it would have been well to have captured Fort Monroe as the fort could not bring half the [Union] guns to bear on her. A land and water attack on Old Point would have captured it, which would have been held for a long time with the aid of the *Virginia,* and Norfolk would have remained in possession of the Confederacy. Another reason for attacking the ships at Newport News was to let the *Patrick Henry, Thomas Jefferson,* and *Teaser* out of James River so they could take part in the fight.

About the middle of March [1862], General [George B.] McClellan was placed in command of the Army of the Potomac and his forces were landed at Old Point. The whole Hampton Roads was covered with shipping loaded with troops and stores, and he advanced slowly up the Peninsula. It took him about two weeks to get to about five miles of Yorktown and then began a slow approach by zigzag breastworks toward that place.

General [John Bankhead] Magruder opposed his [McClellan's] 110,000 men with 11,000, which was kept up until the last of April when he was reinforced by General Joe Johnston, who came from Northern Virginia and took command. After a few skirmishes at Young's and Lee's mills, General Johnston determined to evacuate the Peninsula and draw McClellan up in the country.

We were ordered to Kingsmill Wharf, about four miles from Williamsburg, to assist in the evacuation. We took a load of flour [and] sugar. We had orders to destroy all we could not get on board the schooner. On the wharf was a nice barrel of New Orleans molasses, and as it would be destroyed if left and it was a food that I was always fond of, I rolled it aboard. It was marked "Blassingham, Williamsburg."

At Jamestown we took on several barrels of whiskey and Capt. [Joseph W.] Barlow's battery of artillery of Richmond [the Metropolitan Guards, Tenth Battalion, Virginia Heavy Artillery]. Going up the soldiers knocked the bung out of a barrel of whiskey and sucked the whiskey out through a bayonet scabbard until many of them were drunk.

Brother Billy, who was a member of the Wythe Rifles and had been disabled at Yorktown, was taken up to City Point.

We got a tow up to Richmond from Captain Roberts of the tug *David Curry.* The rain was pouring down in torrents and I took my trick at the wheel steering the steamer. We arrived at Richmond about daylight [on May 4, 1862].

Our troops advanced up the Peninsula and outside Williamsburg the Yankees pressed them too hard, General Longstreet gave them battle [at Williamsburg on May 5] and checked their advance. The fight was a sharp one.

The old man at Williamsburg, Blassingham, was said to be a queer man. He is the man who owned the molasses I rolled on the schooner to save. It is said that when the enemy came into Williamsburg he and his friend, Robert Bright, were scouting around in the woods when they heard a noise in the woods. Mr. Bright called out, "Don't shoot. I surrender." Then Mr. Blassingham threw up his hands and said, "Me, too, me too." It [the noise] was only a drove of hogs jumping through the fence that nearly frightened them to death.

The Yankees kept advancing by degrees and our forces retreated until they were within a few miles of Richmond. Our *Merrimack* or *Virginia* could not be taken up James River on account of the draft of water, so the officers said, so was blown up [on May 11, 1862] at Craney Island, and thus finished one of the greatest naval structures of the world. This was a great loss to the Confederates and the loss was laid unjustly on the pilots. The pilots stated she could not be brought up as far as Jamestown without taking out her guns to lighten her to eighteen feet, which was correct, and without armament the Federals could capture her. We people thought she could have defended the James River at Goose Hill, just below Jamestown. After the ship was blown up the balance of the fleet—*Patrick Henry, Thomas Jefferson, Beauford, Raleigh,* and *Teaser*—went up the James and anchored under the guns of Drewry's Bluff.

A naval court of inquiry was had by request of Admiral [Josiah] Tattnall, the commander of the [ironclad] ship, and he endeavored to throw all the blame on the pilots; but the court decided that the admiral was justified in destroying the ship as to take off her battery to lighten her would expose her to the enemy's shots and she could not be brought up over the flats near Jamestown. The batteries on the river—*viz.* Day's Point, Harden's Bluff, Mulberry Island, and Jamestown—were abandoned.

The Yankee Fleet at City Point

"Musket Balls Whistled Around Lively"

Robert C. Wood's schooner, the *James Buchanan,* was confiscated and used in a pontoon bridge across the James River above Drewry's Bluff, and he and George returned to City Point just days before the Union fleet came upriver. In a dramatic move, Richard Curtis's teenage sister convinced Commander John Rodgers aboard the USS *Galena* that only "peaceable people" inhabited the village, and the warships moved upstream. On May 15, Confederate artillerymen stopped the Union fleet before Drewry's Bluff and Rodgers returned to City Point to repair his damaged fleet.

In a gesture of goodwill, Rodgers sent a surgeon ashore on a mercy mission, but the party was ambushed in "a mean attack" by a contingent of Georgia infantrymen who captured nine Union soldiers. In

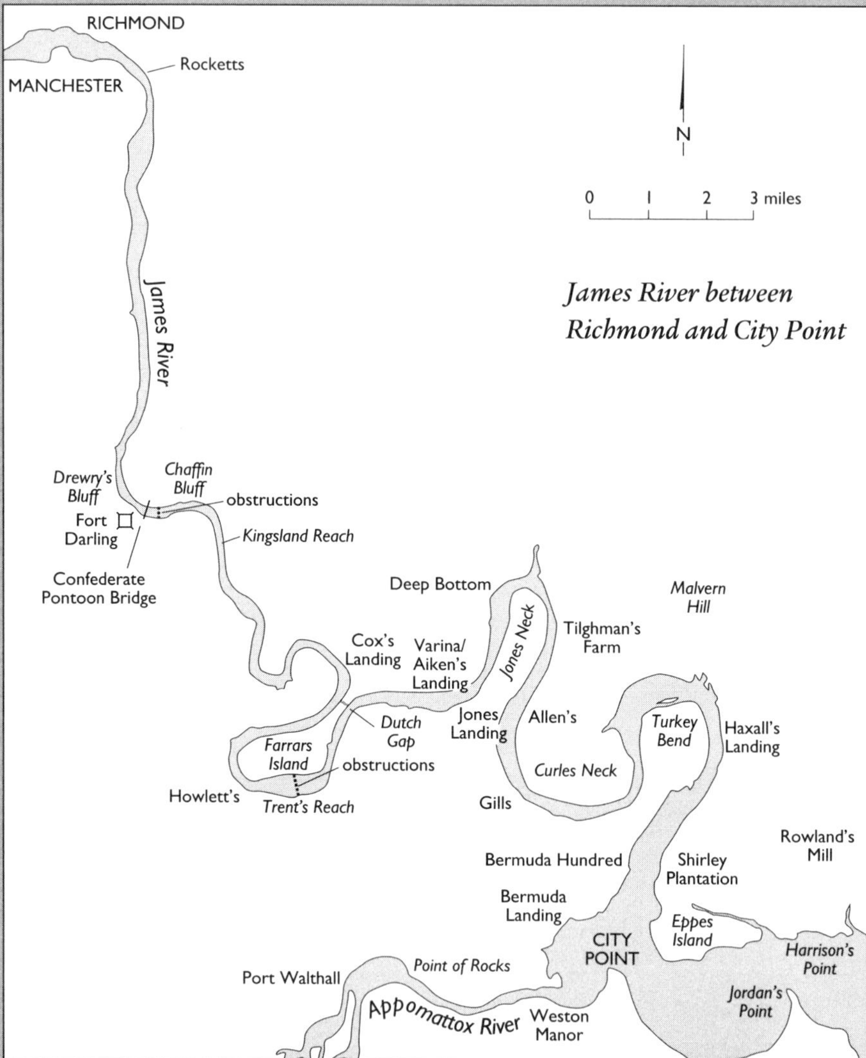
James River between Richmond and City Point
RICHMOND
MANCHESTER
Rocketts
N
0 1 2 3 miles
James River
Drewry's Bluff
Chaffin Bluff
obstructions
Fort Darling
Confederate Pontoon Bridge
Kingsland Reach
Deep Bottom
Jones Neck
Malvern Hill
Tilghman's Farm
Cox's Landing
Varina/ Aiken's Landing
Dutch Gap
Jones Landing
Allen's
Turkey Bend
Haxall's Landing
Farrars Island
obstructions
Howlett's
Trent's Reach
Curles Neck
Gills
Rowland's Mill
Bermuda Hundred
Shirley Plantation
Bermuda Landing
Eppes Island
CITY POINT
Harrison's Point
Port Walthall
Point of Rocks
Jordan's Point
Appomattox River
Weston Manor

response, Union warships fired on the village and homes were invaded. Robert C. Wood and other families from Hampton decided to leave City Point.

When we got to Richmond we were informed that the vessels of the transportation company would be put in a pontoon bridge across the James River about six miles from the city near Drewry's Bluff—and we were out of a job. Several months previous, a battery was built to strengthen Drewry's Bluff and obstructions [were] laid in the river, and when we passed through it was only wide enough in the river for a steamer to pass. The schooner was [used for part of] a pontoon bridge at Warwick [Bar] near Powhatan place on James River.

We loaded [into] Captain [William] Curtis's oyster skiff and Captains Curtis, Massenburg, Wood, and two Wood boys [George and Sam], [with] two Prince George men rowed down from Richmond to City Point that night—about forty-five miles. I was so stiff could hardly stand. We had a quiet rest for several days. A [locomotive] engine was kept at the Point fired up expecting the Yankee gunboats up the river, and [it was to] go on to Petersburg when the fleet appeared.

One morning the flag-of-truce boats, *Northampton,* Captain Hicks, and *Curtis Peck,* Captain Barnes, returned from the lower James where they had taken a load of Yankee prisoners [for exchange], passed the U.S. fleet at Harrison Bar and [when] they passed City Point [on May 13] said the Yankee fleet is coming.

Several of the boys in gray were home on furlough and walked with sticks but at the sight of the [Union] fleet threw their uniforms in the well, buried their guns and threw away the sticks.

We had a clear view of the ships coming up slowly often running aground on account of bad pilots. The tobacco warehouse [owned by a Mr. Wennenburg] was fired and the [railroad] engine (Robert Moody, engineer) went on to Petersburg. When the fleet was off Jordan's Point, five miles, some of the people thought the fleet would see the warehouse on fire and might think the place was fortified and shell us. So one young lady (Miss [Mary] Curtis, now Mrs. W. T. Daougherty) offered to go down on board the ships to inform the commanding officer of the true [nonhostile] state of affairs. So she sat in the stern of a boat with white flag flying and was poled down to the ships by an old veteran of the Mexican War named Tyler. The lady was kindly received by Commodore Rodgers, and they drank wine together, and the commodore gave her a letter to the inhabitants of City Point stating that he was at war only with those people who were at war with them and all peaceable people should be protected.

The ships came up easily enough now right in the channel. They were the *Galena,* flag ship, *Seminole, Aroostook, Naugatuck,* and first *Monitor.* We all suspected old man Tyler was piloting them up. The old man was a pensioner of the Mexican War and a strong Union man. We never saw him again and supposed he went away with them.

At 7 bells, 11½ o'clock, the command was given on the [USS] *Galena,* flagship, to let go port anchor [at City Point]. The lady was put in the gig with the commodore, a young officer and crew, and rowed ashore. When they got into the boat the crew mounted the rigging and cheered her, which was answered on the wharf by the crowd there.[22]

22. The meeting of "a young lady" from City Point with John Rodgers aboard the USS *Galena* is mentioned in the *Official Records of the Union and Confederate Navies in the War of the Rebellion.* Mary Curtis, the eighteen-year-old daughter of Captain William Curtis, was among the contingent of evacuees from Hampton. Her brother, Richard, was a gunner on the CSS *Virginia.* In 1866 she married William T. Daoughtery of Hampton, who served as a cavalryman under Jeb (James Ewell Brown) Stuart. Mary Curtis Daoughtery

Rodgers asked [those of us at City Point] for a pilot. He offered as much as $1,000 in gold to one pilot. They could not do it. They had pledged their word to Governor Letcher to aid this state. He said he would not force any one. He had pilots but they had not been up the river for years. He left at 1 o'clock [on May 14] and at 4 anchored at Varina or Aiken's place on the James. The next day [May 15] he was before Fort Darling and made a big fight, but was beaten off badly damaged.

If he had had good pilots he could have gone up James River past the obstructions that evening and been in the rear of their batteries. The way had been left open for the flag-of-truce boats, but between 3 o'clock and 10 [on May 13] they had sunk [scuttled] the *Northampton, Curtis Peck,* and a schooner belonging to David Curry, and had mounted one more gun on the works and overlook. That morning the *Merrimack* [CSS *Virginia*] crew arrived [by train] from Norfolk to man the guns. What an escape Richmond had, and only for the want of a good pilot it would have been captured in May 1862.

In the [Federal] retreat down the river many of the sailors were killed by sharpshooters off the hills as they passed down—several killed at the lookout masthead. They would be fired down on and before the ships could get off [shore] so as to get the range of the hills, the Southern men would be gone. They

---

died in 1924, and her obituary noted that she "loved the Confederate cause and took an active and keen interest in every good movement for the Confederate soldiers."

George Wood was uncertain identifying the Union warships. The name of the gunboat *Seminole* is crossed out and the name *Keystone* inserted. The *Seminole* was then stationed in Hampton Roads to guard Norfolk. There is no confirmation of a ship named *Keystone* being in the vicinity.

Wennenburg's warehouse was apparently set on fire deliberately to prevent Union capture of tobacco stores.

The identity of Tyler, the Union sympathizer who rowed Miss Curtis to the USS *Galena,* is unknown.

View of City Point, James River, Virginia, August 12, 1862. (Virginia Historical Society, Robert Knox Sneden Diary, Mss5:1 Sn237:1, vol. 3, p. 359)

threw many of their immense shells around the hills, but did no damage except to the trees. Many of them would be cut in two.

So many men were killed at the mastheads that they had to have iron cases put up at the masthead to protect the men. They returned and anchored at City Point. It was said the *Galena* had twenty-seven shots in her. They were repairing for a week.[23]

On Saturday [May 17] the commodore [Rodgers] came on shore; he had a mark on his cheek made by a splinter during the fight [at Drewry's Bluff]. Captain Curtis told him that his wife's sister, Mrs. [Sarah F.] Hopkins, was quite sick, and he said he would send a surgeon on shore Sunday afternoon to see her.

23. The U.S. warships, led by the ironclads *Monitor* and *Galena,* moved up the James River and on May 15 were stopped at Drewry's Bluff where sunken Confederate ships obstructed the channel and artillery fire from Fort Darling caused them to retreat downriver. The *Galena,* the command ship, was severely damaged. Fifteen men were killed and twelve wounded, many from sniper fire from the riverbank. The Confederate victory is credited with saving Richmond.

One of the boys said to be William Minson[24] went to the Confederate camp, about one mile off, and told them the Yankees were coming ashore. The boat [from the USS *Wachusett,* carrying a physician, three other officers, and a crew of eleven] had hardly landed before they were fired on [ambushed by men from the Fourth Georgia Regiment of Volunteers] and compelled to surrender. The [Union] coxswain of the boat was wounded, but escaped in his boat [back to the *Wachusett*]. Sam Wood came near being shot as he ran away with his blue academy uniform on.

The musket balls whistled around lively for awhile and the Southern men cheered for Jeff Davis. They carried their prisoners away [Assistant Surgeon George D. Slocum, a Union paymaster, an engineer, a signal officer, and five seamen]. The *Monitor* let go one gun loaded with grapeshot. The *Aroostook* ran up the mouth of the Appomattox River and fired big shells across. The navy did not want to hurt any of the houses or people, so fired over or across the land. The report would shake the windows, so many [persons hiding] in the cellar thought that they [the shells] went through the top of the house.

This was a mean attack [by the Confederate soldiers] and was condemned by the citizens there at the Point, and steps were taken to secure the release [of Union prisoners from confinement by the Confederates], but it was never done as the surgeon remained in prison about twelve months and was exchanged at the same place where he was captured.

Jim Turner, at a cessation of the firing, started up the hill with his grip singing, "I am an old soldier just from the war," when off went a shell, and Jim dropped to the earth, [which] caused laughter at such a serious time. [Subsequently,] many houses

24. William Minson, who was about two years older than George Wood, was the son of James Minson, a Hampton harbor pilot.

were broken open while the people were away and robbed by the sailors who had landed. It was not safe after this to remain at City Point.[25]

Encountering Robert E. Lee

"We Took Up the March for Richmond"

Robert C. Wood's family found sanctuary across the James River at Rowland's Mill in Charles City County, but was forced to leave when McClellan's army withdrew eastward from Malvern Hill at the close of

25. The *Official Records* confirm in detail the May 19 incident in which a Union physician, sent ashore from the USS *Wachusett* on an "errand of charity" to treat an ill Southern lady, was captured by a contingent of Confederate soldiers. Three other officers and five seamen accompanying Dr. George D. Slocum were also taken prisoner, apparently without resistance although armed, by members of Company I, Fourth Georgia Regiment. At the river's edge where the Union skiff was tied up, Confederates attacked and killed two men and wounded two others, one fatally, as seamen rowed away to the *Wachusett.* In retaliation, the ironclad *Monitor* and the Union gunboat *Maratanza*—not the *Aroostook*—shelled targets in and near City Point. Appomattox Manor, the mansion of Dr. Richard Eppes where U. S. Grant established his headquarters in 1864, was damaged. Shells landed near Weston, the manor house on the Appomattox River where the Wood family resided in 1863–64.

Attempts by Admiral Louis M. Goldsborough, flag officer of the U.S. North Atlantic Blockading Squadron in Hampton Roads, to secure the immediate release of Slocum and the other prisoners were rebutted by Major General Benjamin Huger, commander of the Confederate Department of Appomattox at Petersburg.

The captain of the *Wachusett,* William Smith, who accompanied Rodgers on his Saturday visit to City Point, was relieved of his command "for neglect" by Navy Secretary Gideon Welles for dispatching the Slocum party ashore. Smith was transferred on May 27 to command a lesser vessel, the steam sloop *Seminole.* Two days later Welles reprimanded Goldsborough for communicating with Huger without permission. In July, Rodgers was transferred to command of the monitor *Weehawken* to blockade Savannah, Georgia.

the Seven Days Campaign. As George Wood hiked toward Richmond he spotted Generals Robert E. Lee and Stonewall Jackson, witnessed a soldier's clever theft of a goose, and picked his way across a corpse-strewn battlefield.

All the people moved across the [James] river in flat boats to an island [actually a peninsula, although routinely called an island] belonging to Dr. Eppes, containing about 1,200 acres of land with a house for the overseer and a very large barn. There were at first nine families, to wit: Robert Wood, William A. Wood, Jim Turner, Jim Minson, Charles Topping, Richard Bully, James Massenburg, Robert Pope, and William Curtis.

We divided off the barn by curtains and cooked outdoors under the trees. The first night it was warm, and a young lady slept with her head near the door. An old mule feeding around put his head near in the door, blowed his breath in her face and gave a snort and brayed. She awoke with a scream, and all thought the Yankees had come.[26]

The next morning we cooked with our old fashioned spits under the trees and we looked like a camp of gypsies. We hauled the seine one day to get some fresh fish.

Mr. Wood [Robert, George Wood's father] had a Newfoundland dog named Milton after Milton Johnson of Hampton, and the boys had quite a good time hunting muskrats on the island.

Rebecca Topping's little girl, nine years old, had three small dogs, Fannie, Hector, and Go-fetch-him, and she would alarm the camp if one of the dogs was missing.

William Wood and the Massenburgs got passage home to Hampton.[27] Bully and Curtis went to Westover. Toppings went

26. Elsewhere, George Wood identifies "the young lady" as his sister, Sallie.

27. George Wood's brother, William, was married to Melissa Massenburg.

to Coggin's Point [to Edmund Ruffin's place on the southern side of the James River], Robert Wood went to Rowland's Mill; Minson and Turner to Berkeley. We were compelled to leave the barn as I was down with pneumonia. Dr. Tabb, who occupied the old brick house at City Point, left a lot of medicine at the house and also a copy of Dr. Rush's of Philadelphia works which we brought away with us. They used the cantharides plasters on my side first and then used the other medicine until I got better, and when we got a doctor three days later he said I was all right, [but] advised us to leave.

We got a house near Rowland's Mill and started a crop for the second time that year. The house was situated about one mile from the mill to the west, one mile from Westover to our south, and about two hundred yards from the river road to Charles City Courthouse. (Mr. Rowland was a Northern man but remained neutral.)

About ten days after being settled in the new house one night we heard the cavalry passing on the road up to Richmond. We heard at Mr. Rowland's next day it was General [Jeb] Stuart's men who had passed around McClellan's army. This was a singular situation for the Yankee army to be in. Their gunboat in the James was to the left of his army with only a few miles of country intervening that was traversed often by the Confederates, and Stuart's raid around his army should have taught him [McClellan] the danger of his position.

The Seven Days fight was in a northwesterly direction and was seen by the flash of cannons at night and distant rumbling sound like thunder far off. Tuesday afternoon, July 1, the can-

---

They eventually returned to Hampton. Elsewhere, Wood says returning family members included "Mrs. R. B. Wood and two children," which would have been his sister-in-law, Sarah Phillips Wood.

non roared incessantly. It was at Malvern Hill, about four miles off. Five Yankee troopers rode into our yard and asked the way to Harrison's Landing, and after directing them, we asked what news of the battle.

"Oh," said they, "we are giving the Rebels hell."

"Then why are you retreating?" we asked, and they replied it is "a change of base." They afterward acknowledged it was an awful defeat on the whole Seven Days fight though they were getting the best of the Southern men at Malvern Hill, and General [William Farquhar] Barry with his one hundred guns checked the Confederates there or McClellan's army would have been destroyed. Millions of dollars worth of stores, equipage was destroyed [at White House Landing on the Pamunkey River].

The next day it rained hard and the whole of or what was left of McClellan's army was encamped in our neighborhood. Colonel Owen of Rhode Island was stationed in our yard. The colonel [most likely Captain Charles D. Owen, 1st Rhode Island Artillery] had our downstairs room.

Thursday, General Stuart with his artillery attacked the Yankees in the woods in front of our house, and the shells were thrown over lively. We had to vacate and went to the left over a field to a mill pond. I had a bag of clothing in my hand expecting to return that way and threw it in a fodder house. When we got to the pond, we found a boat filled with water. The boat was bailed out with our hats and while bailing seven of Wade Hampton's cavalry rode down. We told them who we were and showed them where the Yankees were. They rode back and had a skirmish with them.

We crossed the road to the house of Mrs. Barnett where we found Union pickets and shortly after a brigade camped in the field. It was queer to see so many men in the wheat fields with the bundles of wheat, each man taking a bundle for a pillow. Mrs. Barnett gave us dinner of snap beans and country ham.[28]

A young Confederate soldier named Dwight Partelle had been sick at Mrs. Barnett's, and her daughter nursed him. He got well and married the daughter. He was from Washington, and was afraid of being detected, and his wife was frightened also. Finally he exposed himself and an officer recognized him and sent him home to Washington. We thought the young fellow a villain, but after the war he returned to his young wife and lived several years and died of consumption.[29]

Mrs. Barnett told us if we went to Mrs. Acamon's [probably Ackerman's] through the woods we would be in the Confederate lines. We all urged father to go back to the Rowland house, get our household goods, and return to Hampton. The Union officers also urged him, but could not prevail on him to go. He said if he went home he would have no occupation and he could not pilot as the state had prohibited it, and we had all our houses burnt and could not live in them. Besides he wanted to be in or near Richmond so he could befriend his son, Robert, who would not join the South and in consequence was in prison. So we tramped to Mrs. Acamon's and at 9 o'clock we got supper. We slept in the hayloft that night.

She was a widow with two girls and one boy, the boy in the Charles City troop. She was a Yankee woman and treated us

28. Mrs. Barnett most likely was the wife of Samuel Barnett, a miller, who paid a substitute to serve for him.

29. In another recounting of this story, George Wood identifies Dwight Partelle as being from Maryland, "the son of a well-known Washington man," who "was concealed in the house and was afraid he would be seen and captured by the enemy." "Some of our people think he showed himself designingly as the assistant adjutant general said he would have to send him to Washington to his father's."

well, and I will never forget her dialect when she asked her daughter, Percill, "have you any more apple-sass up-stairs?"

The next morning after breakfast we started for the front to see what the army was doing. First we passed General Stuart's forces of cavalry deployed in a large field. He was attempting to hold a high ridge of land overlooking the enemy which was afterwards abandoned as the enemy sent a small gunboat up Herring Creek and fired across the country, but there was a sharp fight that day.

We passed the middle road and stopped for a moment and saw a general with his staff riding down the road. He was on a small sorrel horse, and we exclaimed, "There is General Lee," which was acknowledged by the officers.

We passed down a short road and on a hill by the side of the road in a tent sat the celebrated Stonewall Jackson. I looked in the tent and there sat the general looking over his map unconscious of the boom of cannon in the distance or of the passing of wagon soldiers. He looked like a second lieutenant by his uniform and reminded me of Dr. Harris, who lived at Bethel a mile from town before the war. He never looked up from the map. It brought to my mind the conversation which I had heard between Mr. John Armistead and Dr. Harris, two of the Virginia Military Institute boys, in 1861 just before the war commenced. Mr. Armistead was acting adjutant when the corps [of cadets] was marching down the street and a brick was thrown at Jackson, who was professor and military tactician. At the time, he turned to look where the brick came from and was rebuked by Jackson, who reminded him that a good soldier never looked to the rear.

He said Jackson was very eccentric and suffered with some nervous trouble. He had stated to him that since the Mexican War when he had served with distinction, he had a creeping sensation up his right arm as though a lizard was crawling up his arm, and he would pump the trough full of water every morning that the artillery horses drank out of (although Virginia Military Institute had no cavalry, but artillery and infantry at that time), [because] he thought that exercising the arm would remedy the trouble.

We passed to the next house owned by Mr. Phillips, a tall large house sitting on a hill, and in the yard—grass lawn—stood General Lee in his gray uniform coat buttoned up to the throat, pants in the boots, dark eyes, no whiskers but mustache, well formed and no surplus flesh—every inch a soldier—and his eagle eye saw everything around. He was as straight as an arrow with no corpulence. His dark truthful eyes and his open frank face would impress any stranger with his Christian soldier character. He was about five feet ten [inches] and weighed about 180 pounds. I saw him three years later and he was greatly changed—looked haggard, old, and corpulent.

While we were standing there firing had commenced. General Stuart had attacked the right flank of the enemy and so big guns were fired. He gave some directions to an aide who went upstairs. He reported he could not see, and General Lee said to get out of the dormer window and [get] to the top of the house. The aide returned and reported the heavy firing was from a gunboat of light draft that went up Herring Creek next to Westover and [was] firing at Stuart's men. The firing soon ceased and the attack drawn off.

We left and started for something to eat. Strong people said they were destitute, but we saw them selling biscuits to the soldiers for ten cents a piece.

In the road a large flock of geese were picking grass and an old woman was watching. Along came a soldier with a pin hook attached with a grain of corn. He dropped the corn and one of the geese swallowed it. He ran pulling the old goose with him, and the old woman could not see the string for the dust and thought the goose was chasing him.

The old woman hollered, "Don't run from de goose. He ain't going to hurt you."

The soldier turned the corner of the fence, took out his jack knife and cut off the head of the goose and put him in his bag, and I bet he had a good square meal.

Our next stopping place was at the home of an old man named Moss, about sunset third of July. The "Old Bishop" he was called, and he had a son, T. V. [Thomas Vernon] Moss, who was in the jewelry business in Hampton and in the Grays as third lieutenant. He took us in and gave us supper after a *long* prayer. [This was] after he had fed all the soldiers he could furnish with biscuits at 10c each. We returned soon after supper next morning, 4th July. It was about 9 o'clock before we got anything to eat except a few green apples in the orchard that liked to have killed me. We remained there two days with two meals a day and prayers four times a day through which we paid him in Virginia state money about twice as much as it was worth. He was often abusing the Hampton people for being lazy.

Then we took up the march for Richmond, about twenty miles. There was father, mother, three grown sisters [Martha, Keturah, and Sallie] one 11-year-old girl [Emma], boys, 12 [Edward], 15 [George], and 17 [Sam], and a 15-month-old boy that had to be carried in our arms. We took turns carrying the child [Jefferson Ward Wingfield, George Wood's nephew]. We stopped one night at Crenshaw's, and the next day was very hot and had to pass over the Malvern Hill battlefield, and the stench of dead horses was fearful. Bodies of men were also laying on the ground with the dirt thrown on them and often the toes were not covered up—buzzards were thick and water scarce. Sallie rested for a moment in a fodder house but looking around saw the naked arm of a man that had been cut off that frightened her badly.

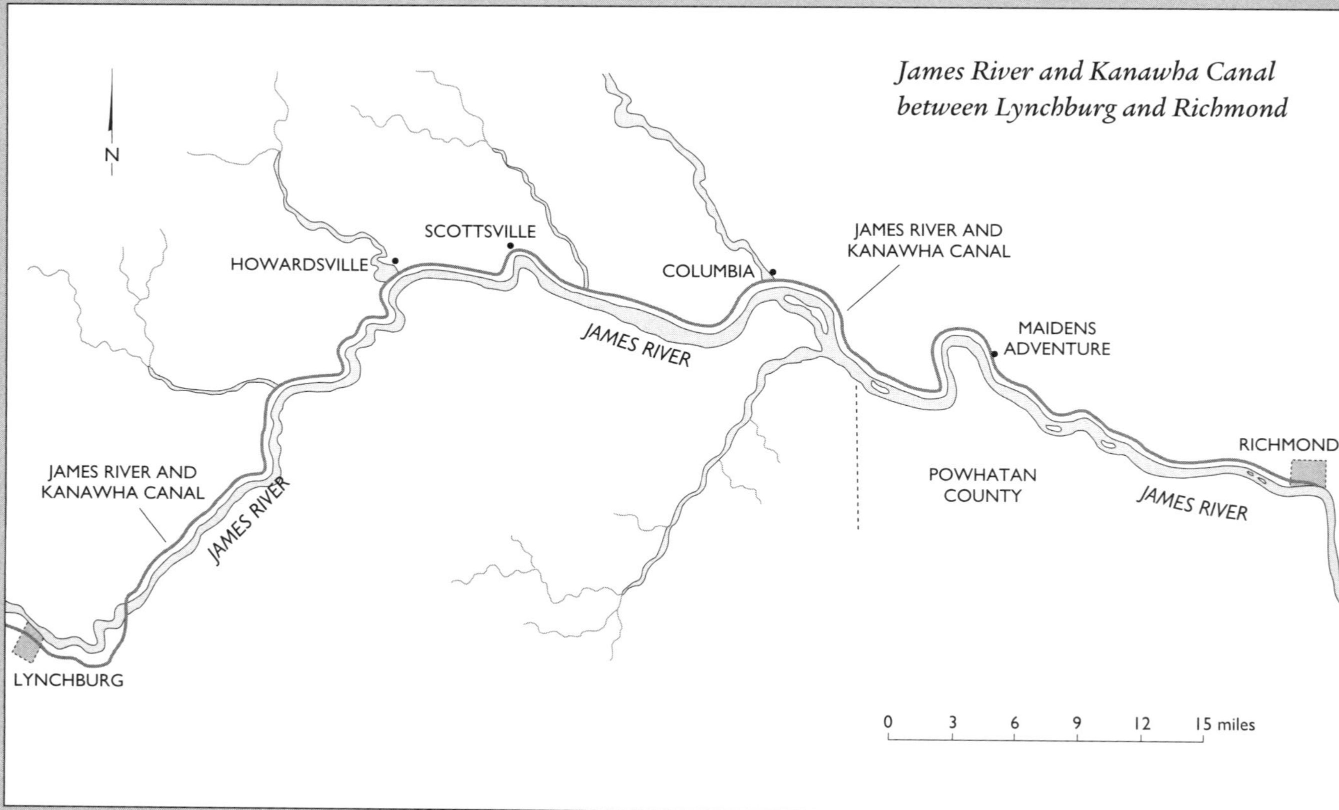
James River and Kanawha Canal between Lynchburg and Richmond
N
HOWARDSVILLE
SCOTTSVILLE
COLUMBIA
JAMES RIVER AND KANAWHA CANAL
MAIDENS ADVENTURE
JAMES RIVER
JAMES RIVER AND KANAWHA CANAL
JAMES RIVER
POWHATAN COUNTY
RICHMOND
JAMES RIVER
LYNCHBURG
0 3 6 9 12 15 miles

Sam picked up an old six-barrel pistol on the field. It was what we called a pepper box—barrels long all around like a pepper box.

When we got about ten miles from Richmond—just about 3 o'clock—we made a friend of Mr. [E. G.] Ghio, wagon-master. He was a Portsmouth man and after the war agent of Bay Line steamers at Portsmouth. (He died in '93.) He gave all the family a ride to Richmond except Sam and I, who later on got a ride in another wagon to within five miles of Richmond. We slept in the wagon and visited the battlefield of Seven Pines and found large quantities of fry pans with bayonet holes stuck in them and other large quantities of camp equipage destroyed [and] buried in great pits.

Working aboard a Canal Boat

"A New Kind of Sailor"

The Wood family set up housekeeping in Richmond and Robert C. Wood got a job operating a freight boat on the James River and Kanawha Canal. George accompanied his father on several trips until he became ill and rejoined his mother and siblings, who had moved from their rented rooms to live aboard the *Plume*, docked at the waterfront. A family friend in the Confederate transportation department assigned George a cargo barge, called an "ark," to deliver supplies to military wharfs along the James River. He was accompanied by a black crewman, Henry Richards, and together they earned money by selling driftwood for fuel and fish caught with a seine.

We found the family [in Richmond] located on Church Hill where they had two rooms in a house rented to Mr. G. B. West [most likely George Benjamin West of Hampton and Newport News Point]. We borrowed two feather beds, bought a

"Confederate troops on a canal freight boat" on the James River and Kanawha Canal, from *Harper's Weekly,* September 28, 1861, p. 616. (Mariners' Museum)

stove, a few chairs and table, knives, forks, and dishes and went into housekeeping again.

We applied to Captain [John Alexander] Curtis, who never went back on a Hampton man, for places, and father got a boat to run on the [James River and Kanawha] canal, and I went on the first trip. I found that this was a new kind of sailor.[30]

30. Freight boats on the James River and Kanawha Canal were the largest carriers of cargo in Virginia in 1860, capable of transporting 80 tons, but seldom exceeded 60 tons. Passenger traffic, however, was not extensive and limited to six packet boats. After the Civil War all waterborne traffic declined rapidly in favor of railroads.

We had two drivers and two steersmen and a cook beside our captain, four mules, two in the back and two on the boat in a stable forward. A driver would drive twelve miles and he and mules would rest twelve miles the same with the steersman who steered twelve miles and rested twelve miles. There were locks to go in every five miles and we went up the canal as the water level grew higher and higher. Our new mules came near being drown at Columbia, but we got them out all right.

Another thing the steerer was required to do was to blow the horn [signaling] to the lockman to open the gates, and the man said, "Open the gates—open the gates—open the gates—open the gates—open-the-gates."

The directions to me about steering into a lock were like Greek. For instance, in a dark night the cook who snubbed or checked the boat going in the locks would say "berm bank" or "tow path" when I had been used to starboard and port. "Tow path" was on the left and "berm bank" was right. I gave up steering and rode or drove the mules. I would ride until sore and walk until tired.[31]

We passed Columbia, Scottsville, Howardsville, and other small places. Two of our mules rebelled and got into the canal, but we got them out. A Negro fell overboard; father tossed him a rope and pulled him in.

A freight would run to Lynchburg, one hundred forty-four miles, in a week, and a packet boat with three horses on a trot would make it in three days. The packet boats had fresh horses at different stables on the route as they wanted all the room on the boats for the passengers. These were filled up with passenger steamer berths, dining room, and kitchen.

31. The tow path was 12 feet wide; locks were 100 feet long and 15 feet wide. The canal was on the north side of the James River between Richmond and a few miles below Lynchburg where it crossed over to the south side.

The boat going up would stop and let the down boat pass over the tow line.

We went up as far as Howardsville loaded with corn and came back. The morning was beautiful to see the James River rolling down over the rocks with the early sun rising out of the mist and the mountains looming up all around us.

Our next trip was to Maidens Adventure, twenty-seven miles up, for wood. This is where the river is dammed up and we got out of the locks into the river at Meacham's Ferry. I left my pair of mules on the north bank of the river and poled the boat across. I had to cross the river every morning in a bateaux[32] to feed the mules and crossing under the falls at sunrise was beautiful with the sun shining on the falls. One would think that the boat would either be drawn under the falls or washed down the river, but it was neither as the falls formed an eddy when the water fell and a boat could be pushed across in this eddy.

This is in Powhatan County—black soil for the cultivation of tobacco, which is a very pretty growth. Tradition says that an Indian maiden loved a white hunter, but her father, the chief, forced her to marry an Indian brave, and she got herself over a hill and threw herself to the rocky river and was drown.

At other places going up the canal the scenery would be great with the high rocky hill and trees on one side, the low land on the other with the river rolling down over the rocky riverbed. Springs sprouted up along the route gushing forth cold water.

I was taken sick with dysentery and remained at home. We had to move from Church Hill and not finding a suitable place to live moved on the pilot boat *Plume* while she lay in the ship dock at the first basin, or slip. The department had hired a man in my place on the [canal] boat, so I went to work for Mr. Thomas, the wharf-builder, to make a screw boat dock in the

32. A lightweight, flat-bottomed river boat with tapering ends.

canal. This is made by driving three rows of piles ten feet apart and capping the top, putting a log crosswise ten feet apart at the bottom, and across up the beam after the boat is put over it.[33]

About this time, August 1862, I visited the captain of the 32nd Virginia [Regiment camped at Chaffin's Bluff] and saw many of the boys who belonged to the Wythe Rifles and Hampton Grays.[34] Some of them I was destined never to see again. We saw [Private] Alex Wood, and he told us of the killing of his brother Nathan in the Seven Days fight. He was a cannoneer at the time and was thought to have been shot by Georgia soldiers by mistake. We never saw Alex again. He was killed at Sharpsburg in that bloody cornfield when the regiment fought so

33. The "screw boat dock" George Wood describes building is a structural platform used to dry dock boats, a shiplift. Gallows-type structures were erected a boat-length apart and a submerged platform was attached over which the boat would be floated; the platform holding the boat was then raised out of the water by a screw mechanism.

34. Among his random journal entries, George Wood inserted this story, which he must have heard repeated many times by reminiscing Confederate veterans.

> When the boys of the 32nd Virginia were stationed at Petersburg in 1862 on a certain night several of the singers in the Hampton companies went out to serenade a very popular young lady named Miss Maloy. At that time the song "Sweet Evalina" was very popular and this was the song selected by them for the serenade, but in the chorus they substituted "Sweet Kate Maloy" for "Sweet Evalina." Arriving at the street on which Miss Maloy resided they stopped in front of one of the houses in the row and filled the air with the melody. After they had about finished, a window was raised and an old gentleman leaned out and shouted:
>
> "Miss Kate Maloy,
> Miss Kate Maloy,
> Miss Kate Maloy
> Lives three doors below."
>
> After which he shut down the window with a bang.
>
> It is needless to say that the boys moved on, no doubt disgusted at the thought that their musical effort had fallen upon such unsympathetic ears.

hard. Others killed were Lt. James Dye, instantly at the head of the company, Sam and William Face, Alex Armistead, Charles Booker.[35]

Captain [John A.] Curtis, who was manager of the water transportation under Maj. Kensey Johns, son of Bishop [John] Johns, gave me command of a large tobacco ark[36] called *John Letcher.* Major Johns was one of the best men I met during the war, very kind and courteous to all. Capt. Joe Scott was put on the *William L. Goggin.*

The *John Letcher* was built for the purpose of offloading ships on the river when they had to finish their loads low down the river on account of the [sand]bars. She would take the balance of the loads down the river to these ships. She would hold sixty cord of wood. These boats were built during the canvass for governor when Letcher was elected in 1860. They were sharp head and square stern so as to put the stern to the wharf to load with flour or tobacco and also to roll them on board of ships.

Richmond had a large trade to Bremen, Germany, for tobacco and to Brazil with flour when the arks were built. Ships would take on part of their load in Richmond and drop down the river beyond the bars in the river and these arks would be loaded and towed down through them so they could finish loading.[37]

35. Casualties at the September 17, 1862, Battle of Sharpsburg/Antietam for the Thirty-second Virginia Regiment were significant: 15 killed outright and 57 wounded. Dye and Sam Face were killed on the battlefield; Armistead and Booker died of wounds. William Face died in January 1864 of chronic diarrhea.

36. A name applied during the first half of the nineteenth century to small bargelike cargo vessels that were poled or towed (also known as a scow); before the Civil War, arks were commonly used on rivers to float logs and agricultural products downstream on the spring freshet.

37. In 1860, more than 2,100 vessels called at Richmond, including 56 packets from New York City and 39 from Boston. The principal incoming

"The James River and Kanawha Canal, Richmond, Virginia," showing barges in the connector canal, from *Harper's Weekly,* October 14, 1865, p. 653. (Mariners' Museum)

Our first work with the arks was to raise the sunken steamer *Junius A. Brown* that was sunk in the river two miles below the city, which we did under the supervision of Mr. Gill and Mr. Booker, city officers, assisted by master workman Fox. This steamer was slow and nicknamed the *Fidely Idely.* We swept chains under her and fastened them to a beam across the deck

---

cargo was coal, barrels of fish, guano, hay, iron, lime, oats, plaster, and sacks of salt. The principal outgoing cargo was barrels of flour, packages of tobacco, and bushels of wheat.

The James River was navigable to the port of Richmond, at Rocketts below the falls, for ships of 1,000 tons with a draft of 11½ feet. Vessels needed a 15-foot draft to clear the Warwick Bar, which was five miles below Richmond. Below City Point vessels could be loaded to a draft of 17 feet.

of mine and another boat at low water. When the tide rose we swung her off the bottom and took the steamer further inshore. It only took three tides to get her lifted so the hole in her side could be stopped, and she was then hauled out at the [ship]ways.

We only had one man besides ourselves on each ark. I had a good man with me named Henry Richards, a yellow man[38] but strong who did his work well.

My first trip was to Mill Rock or Howlett's or Pull-and-be-Dammed for a load of wood. The place was on the bend of the [James] river at the upper part of Trent's Reach and very narrow.

None of our people see the place now going up the James as it is above Dutch Gap. We called it Mill Rock on account of an old mill once there at its rocky jagged hills. The sailors called the place "Pull-and-be-Damned" because the high rocky hill would break off the wind from the sails and the vessels would have to be towed around the rocky point by a boat at the head of the vessel. It was to avoid this narrow bend, together with the advantage getting seven miles nearer Richmond that caused General Butler to cut through the narrow gap called Dutch Gap in 1864, which route is used to this day.

I arrived there about 12 o'clock and went up to the large dwelling house on top of the hill. Mr. Howlett invited me in a large room where he and a gentleman were and invited me to take a drink. I took one to be social, but did not like it.

This house is one of the highest parts of the navigable James. When the Confederates had their battery in 1864, and lines of defense running across the [Bermuda Hundred] Peninsula, the house was riddled by bullets but survived the war and was burnt in 1893. Chestnuts, sloves [wild plums], and grapes were abundant. Partridges had been plentiful but the North Car-

38. A person of mixed race.

olina soldiers had trapped them, so an old darkey told me. He made a trap on shore with his seine. He would catch birds or fish. He went fishing every day, but one day laid down under the shelving rocks in his boat where it was shady and went to sleep. The tide was low and soon arose, caught the boat against the rocks, filled it with water and drown him. He was buried in the valley below.

Wild ducks, rabbits, squirrels, turkeys were plentiful, but there were few gunners and no shot. The only kind of shot we could get was homemade—lead cut in strips or beat out long and cut into slugs that would fly in every direction when shot out of a gun. In fact, most of the gunners (soldiers) used larger shot (bullets) and were after larger Blue Birds (Yankees). We would now and then kill a duck, goose, and catch catfish to make chowder.

Henry Richards foraged around the country and got vegetables to eat. He also was a good fisherman and as soon as the boat stopped he would throw over his line and catch a catfish, but it was a year or more before I could get used to eating catfish because we had been used to such superior fish in Hampton.

Henry would gather all the driftwood which we had the privilege to carry to the amount of two cords which brought us $12.00 profit. Each trip we often brought corn and doubled our money. One day a fisherman left his seine with us and we caught 120 shad in two tides. We sold eighty for $1.00 each, Confederate money, and salted forty for home. We often made extra money and would be greeted with loving smiles through tears when I gave it to mother. I only kept a few dollars for tobacco and to attend the theater [in Richmond].

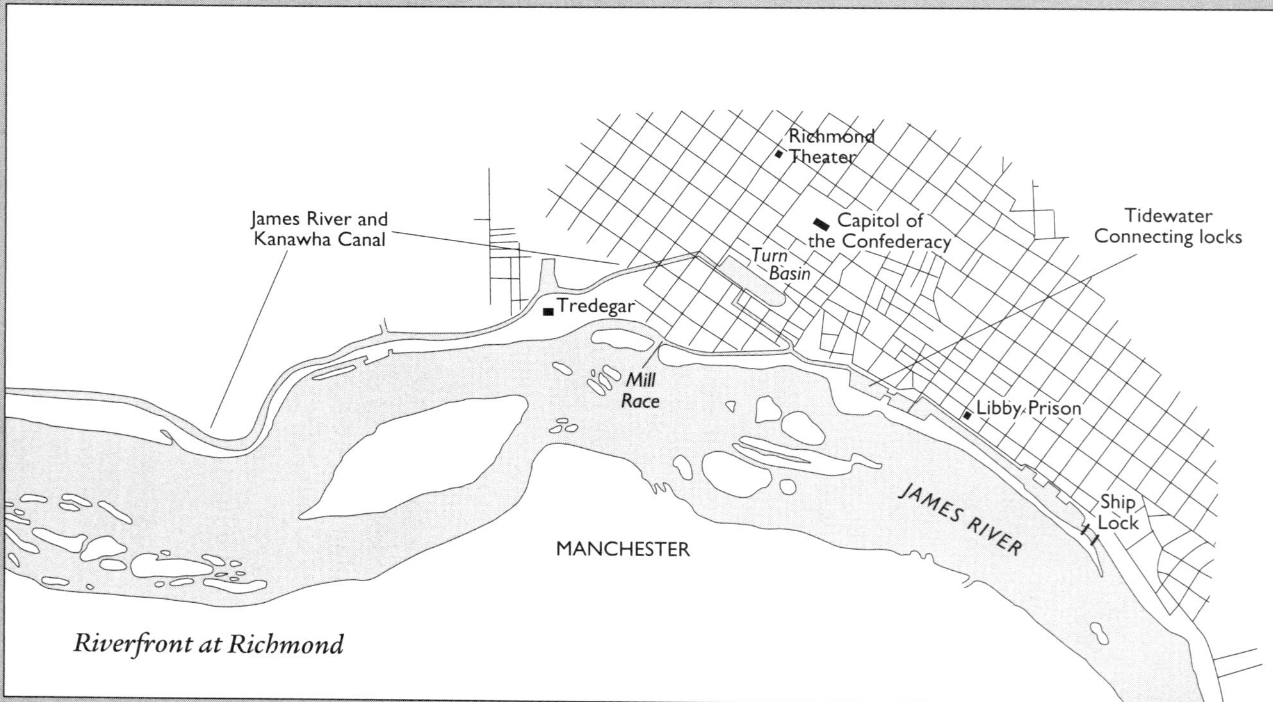

Riverfront at Richmond

Theater in Wartime Richmond

"The Price of a Parquet Ticket"

George was enamored with the theater and at every opportunity attended variety shows, performances of Shakespearean plays, and hastily written dramas of war-related themes that included sham battles intended to boost the morale of Confederate soldiers. He was particularly fond of one singer, Sallie Partington, and years afterward apparently could recite from memory words of songs she sung—and remembered with regret hearing a tune sung by a Union prisoner of war.

We had often attended the theater; first at the old Metropolitan on Franklin Street and afterwards in the new one on the corner of Broad and Seventh streets. It is strange to say that although Grant was burning on one side and Butler on the other side of Richmond, the plays were on like Nero fiddling while Rome was burning.[39]

R[ichard] DeOrsey Ogden was the stage manager. Ogden was said to be an Englishman and had British protection, which kept him out of the army. He had actors Jim Harrison, Jim Wells, F. M. Bates, C[harles] H. Morton, Harry Allen, [a person identified only as] Duncan, J. W. Thorpe, J. W. Warren, [R. J.] Brown. Actresses Sallie and Mary Partington, Katie Estelle, Mrs. C[lementina] DeBarr, Miss Powell, Ella Wren, Miss Taylor.[40]

39. The Richmond Theater at 701 East Broad Street was destroyed by fire on January 2, 1862, and rebuilt on that site, opening on February 9, 1863. The last wartime performance there was given on April 2, 1865.

40. In a letter to the *Richmond Times-Dispatch* written in 1914, George Wood reports: "I remember Tim Morris and Joe Buckley, the minstrels. One night

The plays [by Shakespeare] were *Romeo and Juliet,*[41] *Macbeth, King Lear, Merchant of Venice, Hamlet, Othello.* [Also] *Catherine Howard,* [*The Intrigues of the Court of the*] *Stewarts* [*sic*], *Duel in the Snow, The Virginia Cavalier, The Lady of Lyons.*

In July 1864 Ida Vernon came through the blockade by steamer from Nassau [landing at Wilmington, North Carolina] and brought many new plays such as *East Lynne, Aurora Floyd, Fanchon! the Cricket!* etc. The play of *East Lynne* was too solemn to the soldier boys who were the principal part of the audience. The price of a parquet[42] ticket was $2.00 in Confederate money.

The play of *The Virginia Cavalier* was one of the enlivenly ones and all of the war theme.[43] Bates took the part of Captain Rowland in the Confederate army who was affianced to Susan (Ella Wren), who had been a former sweetheart of the Yankee Colonel Wyndam (Jim Harrison). Sallie Partington was a cousin of Ella Wren. Duncan was a Confederate recruit, Sallie's beau. [Richard D'Orsey] Ogden was the Negro servant of Captain Rowland. The soldiers of the city were drilled to fill up the parts.

The scene opened in a valley surrounded by mountains with a visit by the girls to the Confederate camp and a picnic and dance was held on the green. The heroine was captured, carried to the Yankee camp. Rowland and his servant rescue her by stealing in the camp and bringing her back when crossing the river. The Negro servant was on the Confederate side with the girl while

---

one of our sailors pulled off the coat of the thief that was escaping from the stage in trying to catch him. He did not know it was all in the play. . . . After the war, Jim Harrison, Harry Allen, Katie Estelle, Buckley and Morris played in Hampton."

41. Elsewhere, Wood notes that *Romeo and Juliet* impressed him "so I did not sleep much that night."

42. A place immediately in front of the stage.

43. *The Virginia Cavalier* was written by Captain George W. Alexander, who was in charge of the prison Castle Godwin in Richmond.

Rowland was on the Yankee side of the river and they were so close that he preferred his own capture to the capture of the girl. He cut the bridge away. The scene was beautiful with the moonlight shining on the river. Rowland was then tried as a spy by the Union officers and condemned to be shot when his servant made the Dutch sentinel drunk then let his companion [a Confederate disguised in a Union uniform] take his place while the servant liberated the captain (Rowland). When they had nearly arrived at the Confederate camp, the Yankees pursued, and a battle took place on the stage between the Union and Confederate forces, and the Confederates whipped them off.

During this play Sallie Partington[44] sung several Southern songs of the day such as "The Cot Where I Was Born," "Soldier Boy," "Lone Rock by the Sea," "Cottage by the Sea," but the most favored one sung was "Virginia, Virginia," which I will give a part of:

Virginia, Virginia, the home of the free,
The birthplace of Washington, the land of liberty.
Your soil is invaded by tyrants and knaves;
Your fields once so brilliant, now gloomy with graves.

Virginia, Virginia, the battle has begun.
We've met the Northern army and the victory is won.

44. Forty years after seeing her on stage, George Wood visited Sallie Partington at her home in Fulton, a Richmond neighborhood, and afterwards corresponded with her. In a letter to the *Richmond Times-Dispatch* after her death he recalled: "I told her that her singing of the popular airs 'The Cottage by the Sea,' 'Lone Rock by the Sea,' 'The Cot Where I Was Born,' etc. reminded me of my home beyond the sea that I had left. . . . She sent me a copy of 'The Southern Soldier Boy,' which she sang in Captain Alexander's *The Virginia Cavalier,* as well as several other mementoes of the war. I invited her to visit Hampton, promising to show her the various places of interest in the vicinity, as well as introduce her to a number of the Confederate boys here, but she never came."

Virginia Virginia the battle has begun
We have met the Nothern Army
And the Victory is Won
The Cry of our leader every where shall
On, On to the Charge—#
Yea brave Sons Follow me

Come on ye brave Sires.
And fly to the field
Let Victory be your aim
And Currage be thy sheild
Trust in Your God
For he rules notes us all
Trust in thy maker
Be ready at his Call

I think it would be well to give a verse or two of other Songs as it would interest Some of the young people—I give it from M

When Dahlgreen Came so near Comin Richmond all the men who worked in department & who was organized were ordered out to defend the City and they had on City recruits and Convalencent Soldiers defend it against two or three thous men—Dahlgreen was Killed in Ja City Co and remains brought to Richmond in a Coffin with a glass plate in front all Could gaze on his face—I took a look at him. he was a fine looking man We all Supposed that his remains were sent North at that time but it is reported Sin the War that his remains were Stolen an

Rock me to sleep mother by Ella Wren and she dwells on the words Wood of the hollow base the untrue mother oh mother my heart calls for you I was doing the play of East Lynn then I first heard Then you'll remember me wh Were sad and touching

Another Song
When I was in the army
Then I did not mind
[illegible]

The cry of our leaders ever shall be
On, on to the charge, ye brave sons, follow me.

Come on, ye brave sons, and fly to the field.
Let victory be thy aim and courage be thy shield;
Trust in your God for he rules us all.
Trust in thy maker, be ready at his call.

Another favorite was "Down in Old Virginia":

Nowhere does the corn wave and grow
Nowhere does the mountain rivulet flow
Nowhere do we wander hand and hand, to and fro
  Like way down in old Virginia.

Nowhere does the ivy to the colonial mansion cling
Nowhere do the birds gather and so sweetly sing
Nowhere do prettier girls on shady lawn swing
  Like way down in old Virginia.

Nowhere at evening as the sun sinks in the west
Nowhere does it shine over loved ones gone to eternal rest
Nowhere has a land by God been so richly blest
  Like way down in old Virginia.

Nowhere does the sun rise out of the ocean blue
Nowhere does it reflect in colors of every shade and hue
Nowhere is it so pretty shining on the dew
  Like way down in old Virginia.

It was during the play of *Duel in the Snow* that I first heard the song "Rock Me to Sleep, Mother" by Ella Wren, and she dwelt on the words, "Mother, oh Mother, my heart calls for you."

"Rock Me to Sleep, Mother"

Backward, turn backward, O Time, in your flight,
Make me a child again, just for tonight!
Mother, come back from the echoless shore.

Take me again to your heart as of yore:
Kiss from my forehead the furrows of care,
Smooth the few silver threads out of my hair,
Over my slumbers your loving watch keep—
Rock me to sleep, Mother—rock me to sleep.

Backward, flow backward, O tide of the years!
I am so weary of toil and of tears!
Toil without recompense, tears all in vain;
Take them and give me my childhood again!
I have grown weary of dust and decay,
Weary of flinging my soul-wealth away,
Weary of sowing for others to reap—
Rock me to sleep, Mother—rock me to sleep!

Tired of the hollow, the base, the untrue,
Mother, O Mother, my heart calls for you!
Many a summer the grass has grown green,
Blossomed and faded—our faces between—
Yet with strong yearning and passionate pain,
Long I tonight for your presence again;
Come from the silence so long and so deep—
Rock me to sleep, Mother—rock me to sleep!

Over my heart in days that have flown
No love like mother-love ever has shone;
No other worship abides and endures
Faithful, unselfish and patient like yours;
None like a mother can charm away pain
From the sick soul and the world-weary brain.
Slumbers' soft calms o'er my heavy lids creep—
Rock me to sleep, Mother—rock me to sleep!

At another time a soldier not being satisfied with the playing of an actor threw a chunk of bread on the stage. The actor picked it up, tasted it and said it was good bread, but the man who threw it was very "ill bred."

The people accused Ida Vernon of being a Yankee. One night after the encore she appeared before the curtain and said she had been charged with being a Jersey Yankee, which was false: her father was French and her mother was Irish and she was born on the high seas; and Virginia was the home of her adoption.

Ogden, the manager, took the part of Archibald Carlyle, and when he received the letter from his Lady Isabella informing him of her elopement, he walked across the stage in a dejected manner: an old soldier said he looks like he was going to Camp Winder. Camp Winder was the conscript camp, and he had been carried there that day but got off by claiming British protection.[45]

It was during the play of *East Lynn* that I first heard, "Then You'd Remember Me," which was sad and touching.

There were many other popular songs such as "Who Will Care for Mother Now," "Tramp, Tramp, Tramp, The Boys Are Marching," "Dixie," "Bonnie Blue Flag," "Let Our Brave," "Farewell Forever to The Star-Spangled Banner," "Richmond on the James."

The Federals sang "Sherman Marching Through Georgia," "Rally Around The Flag," "John Brown's Body," "Year of Jubilee," "Coming, Father Abraham," "Hang Jeff Davis on a Sour Apple Tree."

45. In an undated letter to the *Richmond Times-Dispatch,* Wood writes: "I can recall from my personal recollection the shooting affair between Ogden, manager of the Broad Street Theater, and the newspaperman that was witnessed by one of our Hampton business men. The newspaper, which I think was called the *Southern News,* often nagged the actor, and I remember it said that *Macbeth* with a 'k' was played at the theater—referring to an error of type in the program. Ogden was generally disliked because he claimed his British citizenship and would not go to the front. One night when in an Irish play he was made to say 'I will go back to England,' a soldier yelled out, 'You had better go or you will lose your British protection!'"

Old S. M. Gregory, the banjo picker, would often meet at City Point and he used to sing many of the old rebel songs. After the war he would sing the good old rebel songs and poems at home [in Hampton].

I think it would be well to give a verse or two of other songs as it would interest some of the young people.

"Lorena"

Years creep slowly by, Lorena;
The snow is on the grass again;
The sun's low down the sky, Lorena;
The frost gleams where the flowers have been,
But the heart throbs on as warmly now
As when the summer days were nigh;
Oh! the sun can never dip so low
A-down affection's cloudless sky.

A hundred months have passed, Lorena,
Since last I held that hand in mine,
And felt the pulse beat fast, Lorena,
Though mine beat faster far than thine,
A hundred months—'twas flowery May,
When up the hilly slope we climbed,
To watch the dying of the day
And hear the distant church bells chimed.

We loved each other then, Lorena,
More than we ever dared to tell;
And what we might have been, Lorena,
Had but our loving prospered well!
But then, 'tis past; the years have gone,
I'll not call up their shadowy forms;
I'll say to them, Lost years, sleep on,
Sleep on, nor heed life's pelting storms.

The story of the past, Lorena,
Alas! I care not to repeat;
The hopes that could not last, Lorena,
They lived, but only lived to cheat.
I would not cause e'en one regret
To rankle in your bosom now—
"For if we try we may forget,"
Were words of thine long years ago.

Yes, these were words of thine, Lorena—
They are within my memory yet—
They touched some tender chords, Lorena,
Which thrill and tremble with regret.
'Twas not the woman's heart which spoke—
Thy heart was always true to me;
A duty stern and piercing broke
The tie which linked my soul to thee.

It matters little now, Lorena,
The past is in the eternal past;
Our hearts will soon lie low, Lorena,
Life's tide is ebbing out so fast.
There is a future, oh, thank God!
Of life this is so small a part—
'Twas dust to dust beneath the sod,
But there, up there, 'tis heart to heart.

"Lone Rock by the Sea"

O [illegible] not the woods are fair
The spring is on her way.
When will I know how pleasant those
In joy the young lovers play?
How sweet are winds of morn or ere
The violets breath may be.

Oh, ask me love,
My lone rock by the sea.
(repeat last two lines)

"Cottage by the Sea"

Childhood's days now pass before me
Dreams and scenes of long ago
Like a dream they hover over me
Calm and bright as evening's glow.
Days that knew no shade or sorrow
When my young heart was pure and free
Joyful hail each coming morrow
In the cottage by the sea.

Fancy sees the rose trees turning
Around the old and rusty door
And below the white beach shining
Where I gathered shells of yore.
Hear my mother's gentle warning
As she took me on her knee
And I feel again life's morning
In the cottage by the sea.

The last two songs were favorites with refugees from Hampton as they reminded them of home.

The first time I heard the song "Tramp, Tramp, The Boys Are Marching" was in 1863, when taking a load of Federal sick and wounded soldiers down the James River to the flag-of-truce steamer *New York*. We left Richmond at 12 o'clock at night, the men being placed in the bottom of the boat on straw. Capt. Darius Hill of the steamer *Shultz* towed my boat down, and I let a man wounded in the arm sleep in my bunk, and when not sleeping sang the song "Tramp, Tramp, The Boys Are Marching." He left me a reminder in the shape of lice.

Visiting Weston on the Appomattox

"A Leave of Absence"

George Wood continued to operate his ark, saw the effects of a floating mine on a Union gunboat, celebrated Christmas with a goose that Henry shot, and carried Federal prisoners of war for exchange at Aiken's Landing. When his boat was deliberately sunk to block the James River downstream from Richmond, he took leave to visit his parents, who had moved to Weston Manor on the Appomattox River.

He returned to Richmond and was given command of a larger barge, and became trapped at Petersburg on the Appomattox River when the Federal fleet arrived and occupied City Point on May 5, 1864. His family fled Weston Manor and, with the assistance of a Union general, returned to Hampton—an adventure recorded by George's sister, Emma.

Meanwhile, George, accompanied by a barge captain he identified only as Cullory, witnessed—from dangerous vantage points—the June 15–18 Battle of Petersburg, when Wise's Brigade and other outnumbered Confederates rallied to repel Federal assaults and prevent the loss of the city. During artillery bombardments he encountered a frightened Confederate soldier, a deaf tobacco warehouse superintendent, a religious-minded teamster, and General Lee, who was studying a map.

All persons—women, children, all men and boys—could find employment in Richmond at high wages, but it took all they made just to be able to live. Women and girls made clothing, socks, haversacks, sheets, &c. Boys could get work in the Ordnance, Quartermaster and Navy departments, but all who could bear arms were attached to some city company. Many of

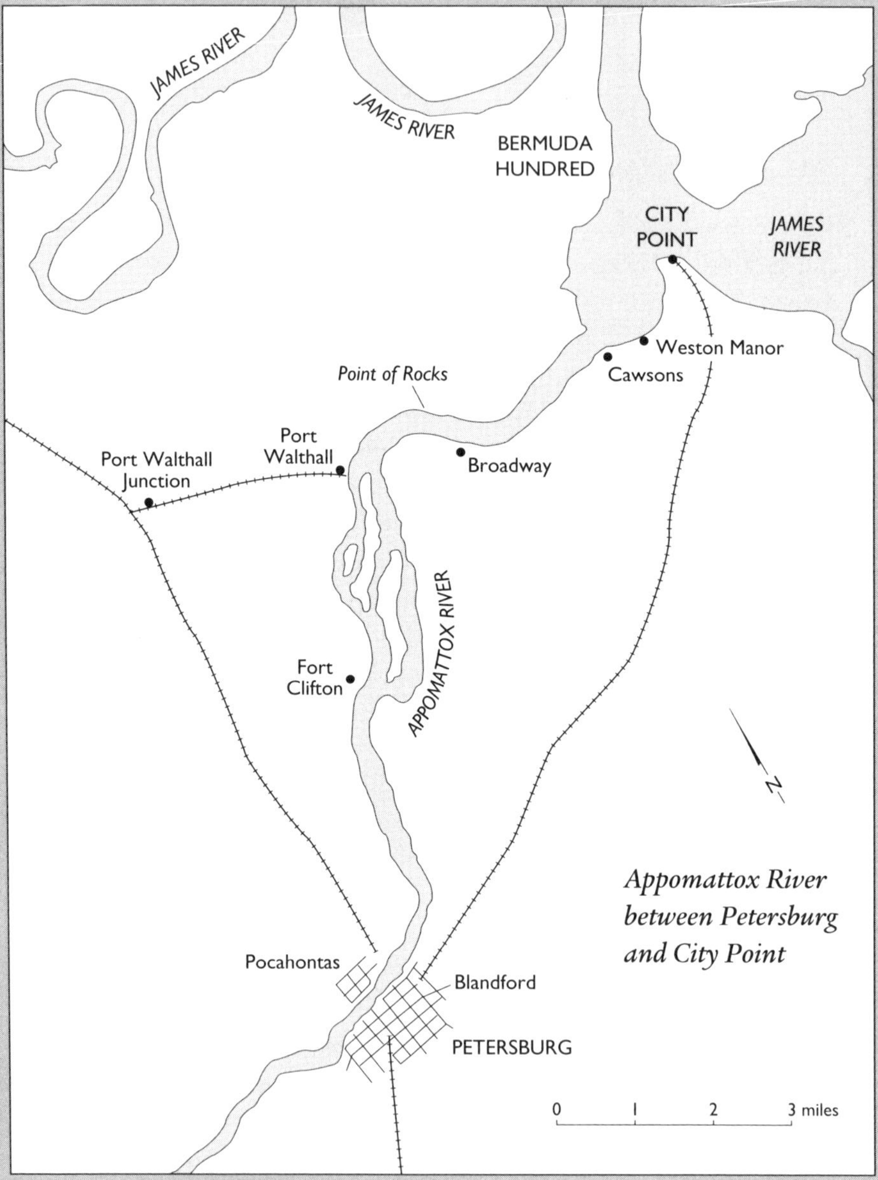

Appomattox River between Petersburg and City Point

our people who had taken refuge in Richmond got work in these departments to support them. We were fortunate in having Mr. D[aniel] G. Murrow as clerk for a short time in the Clothing Department.

I was constantly running wood and hay from different wharfs in the river as low as Wilcox Landing. Mill Rock, Gills, Bermuda Hundred, Curles Neck, Shirley, and Jones [Neck Landing] are some of the places.

One trip I made to Claremont under the care of the gunboat *Beaufort,* Captain William Parker, to take on a load of Maj. William Allen's railroad stock from the small railroad he had running [before the war to carry] wood and lumber through his farms to the wharf for shipment North. The iron was taken to Richmond and [at Tredegar Iron Works] molded for war materials. Cary Mahone was in the Navy and on the gunboat. He was a Hampton boy.

Once when we stopped at Curles Neck where a large sturgeon was caught, and the German steward on the gunboat asked for the roe, which in those days was thrown away. But he made an excellent dish of it, which has since become famous under the name of "caviar."

I made several trips to Watkins Wharf with wood and several loads of hay from Curles Neck, another of Mr. Allen's plantations.

In 1863 the ark was at Shirley Wharf taking on a load of clover hay from the Haxall farm when the U.S. gunboat *Commodore Barney,* side-wheel steamer monitor[46] towed by a gunboat tug, came up the river. I took all my bedding ashore and lay down under the trees as they passed and slept under the trees that night.

General [John Gray] Foster sat under an awning on the deck

46. A generic term for an armored, shallow-draught warship mounting one or two large, turreted guns on a low, flat deck.

"Explosion of a Torpedo under the Bow of the United States Gun-boat 'Commodore Barney' in the James River," from *Frank Leslie's Illustrated Newspaper,* August 29, 1863, p. 357. (William E. Rouse Library, Hampton, Virginia)

of a monitor (could have shot him with my old musket). About two hours afterward heard the boom of the cannon. When they got up as high as Sailors Tavern, the Confederates exploded a torpedo at the bow of the *Barney* a little too soon, and it washed overboard and killed several men and disabled her. The *Washington Tribune* says the *Barney* lost eleven men.

A rocket went up that night, and a fast tug came up next morning and took the *Barney* in tow and towed her down. The vessels came down together, shelling the woods on both sides. The pumps were going on the *Barney* throwing a stream as large as one's body.[47]

47. The USS *Commodore Barney,* while participating on a joint army-navy reconnaissance above Dutch Gap on August 5, 1863, was damaged by the

I expected they [the Union ships] would take or demolish the ark, but did not touch her. The fact that she was at Shirley saved her, as the Federals had agreed to let Hill Carter's property alone as he had been an old army officer and not taking any part in the war. He was also connected with General Lee by marriage. Colonel Carter came to the wharf when the fleet passed up, and regretted my boat was at his wharf. The hay was hauled across his farm to his wharf for shipment.[48]

I was taking on a load of hay at Curles Neck farm when [arrived] an Italian named Tonias, who had been rode on a rail out of the navy yard [in Richmond] because he would not join the army. He was a caulker in the yard. He had stowed himself away and came down, left the next night in one of the small boats down the river to the Yankees. Ten years after the war I met him in Hampton, and he told me he had settled in York County.

I took a load of hay from Drewry's Bluff in November 1863. It was my birthday (fifteen) and it snowed that morning. We had to roll [the hay] down the hill as it was a hundred feet high. We had no trouble to get it down.

I was getting a load of wood at Jones Landing opposite Varina in Christmas week on the 24th. It was snowing hard and Henry, my man, asked for the musket to kill a wild goose; there were [many] flying around and feeding in a wheat field. He was gone

---

concussion of a thousand-pound electric torpedo that Confederates on shore set off prematurely. About twenty men were washed overboard, two of whom where lost. As the *Barney* and two other ships retreated downstream, they encountered heavy artillery fire. The *Barney* was hit more than thirty times and its boiler disabled.

48. In July 1862, General George B. McClellan granted Hill Carter protection owing to "the humane and Christian conduct you and your family have displayed towards my helpless sick & wounded." His father's sister, Anne Hill Carter, was the mother of Robert E. Lee, hence Carter and Lee were first cousins.

Aiken's Landing with barge boats in the foreground.
(Library of Congress, LCID cwpb 01910)

about an hour; when he returned [he had] a fat wild goose for our Christmas dinner.

This is the place [Varina] where the Federals exchanged prisoners during the first part of the war. In 1864 it was General Butler's, or General [Edward O. C.] Ord's headquarters. A pontoon bridge crossed the James at this point and troops could cross the bridge, then march five miles across the country and get to Bermuda Hundred opposite City Point in two or three hours while it would be twenty miles around by the river.

The next day the balance of boats came up, and we were taken [towed] to Richmond. One of the darkies on one of the other boats asked a man for the loan of his pipe as he had not had a smoke for a week. He loaned the pipe but filled the bottom with [gun]powder. When the pipe exploded it frightened the Negro nearly to death.

My father got dissatisfied as his hands (Negroes) were always stealing, and he was not used to lashing human beings, which had to be done; so he resigned and went into the Ordnance

Union troops at Weston Manor in 1864. (Mathew Brady photograph, National Archives, Washington, DC, NWDNS-111-B-2015)

Department. This took him from home nearly all the time, so he gave it up and moved down on the Appomattox River at a place called "Weston" owned by Captain Charles Nelson.[49]

Mr. [Marion] Colbert of our town was in charge of the quartermaster boatyard for the repair and building of canal boats, and I would often meet him. Mr. Thomas Phillips at the corner of 7th and Broad streets, a former resident of this county [Elizabeth City], was often seen by our people, and he treated them hospitably.

49. George Wood's youngest sister, Emma Virginia, claims that their father, Robert C. Wood, felt mistreated and insulted when he was denied a position on a Confederate gunboat because his eldest son, Robert B., was held prisoner in Richmond as a Union spy. Instead, she said, an unidentified oysterman from Hampton who had no piloting experience was commissioned.

In the fall of 1863, Robert C. Wood sold his interest in the pilot boat *Plume* for $500 Confederate money and moved the family to Weston Manor on the Appomattox River. Emma remembered that he spent $200 for two barrels of flour and $50 for shoes made from dog skin, which he gave to her.

Castle Thunder, once a large tobacco warehouse on Cary Street, was a military prison, and Capt. R[ichard] M. Booker [of Hampton] was in command. Libby House was commanded by Captain [George W.] Alexander. Most of the City Battalion did the guard duty there.

Dr. [George William] Semple [of Hampton] had charge of two large hospital buildings on Cary and 27th streets (former tobacco houses), where Union soldiers were treated. In 1863 I took a number of wounded prisoners from Dr. Semple's hospital [aboard the ark] and [was] towed by the steamer *Schultz,* Capt. D. H. Hill, now of the Bay Line. Two died on the way.[50]

We brought back a lot of luxuries—can goods—to the prisoners at the Libby Prison, and the prisoners came on board and got these goods. Many of these goods were broken open before they got from the boat; the prisoners stole from each other.

Major Munford was commissioner of exchange on the Union side and met us at City Point on the steamer *New York.* Colonel Old was the Confederate commissioner.

Between the ship dock or canal and Old Dominion wharf at

50. Elsewhere in his writings, George Wood recalls a conversation overheard in a butcher shop that revealed a coincidental wartime encounter:

> Dick Ruth, the one-legged chief of the Fire Department of the Hampton Soldiers Home and for years in charge of the beer hall on that reservation, was known by nearly everybody in this locality. About twenty-five years ago, while waiting in the meathouse for the butcher to cut up a leg of beef, he remarked to Dr. [George William] Semple, who was standing by, about the doctor sawing off his leg. The doctor asked him where the job was done and Dick replied: "In Richmond."
>
> "Then," said the doctor, "I must have been the man who did it as I was in charge of the Federal Hospital, 25th and Cary streets, at that time."
>
> In thinking over the matter I have no doubt that Captain Hill and myself brought Dick down the James to the flag-of-truce steamer *New York* at City Point, as Captain D. H. Hill in the *Schultz* and my boat, the *Letcher,* brought 125 wounded and convalescent Union prisoners from that hospital in 1863.

The flag-of-truce steamer *New York.* (Library of Congress, LCID 02050)

Rocketts, three large gunboats were built by William A. Graves of Norfolk. They were called *Virginia II, Richmond,* and *Fredericksburg.* They were on the style of the old *Merrimack* or *Virginia* (terrapin shape). They were so heavy after being armored that they could not get over the Richmond or Warwick Bar so our ark was sunk alongside these vessels and timbers run through the portholes across the ark. The holes would be plugged, and water pumped out so as to lighten them a couple of feet while these were used by the navy department.

I was idle, or in the water. I asked for a leave of absence and got it and rode on across to Petersburg and walked to Weston on the Appomattox to see my people. It was in February 1864 and they had a hard time to get something to eat, often living all the week on day-old cornbread—sometimes a duck or muskrat. We sent $50.00 to the mill for a bushel of meal. The miller refused to take $50.00 [in Confederate money]. We sent 50 cents in silver and got the meal.

One day I walked down sixteen miles to see Captain Topping's people at Edmund Ruffin's Beechwood place [at Coggin's Point] on the James River in Prince George County. Captain Topping lived first at Tar Bay, Tommy Cocke's place. It was during the time he lived there [in 1862] that Confederate General [William Nelson] Pendleton mustered about fifty guns on the bank of the river and opened on the Federals [McClellan's army resting across the James at Westover and Harrison's Landing] and made a big stir among them. The next day the Federals [crossed the river and] went into Ruffin's house and marked on the walls "Edmund Ruffin Dam Son of a B— fired the first gun at Fort Sumter." Ruffin committed suicide after the war. These were beautiful places but looked neglected as most of the slaves had gone to the Yankees.

Two boys at home on furlough had captured a schooner one dark night loaded with corn and burnt her. She sank at land and the wild duck would dive down to get the corn, and the Topping boys placed a blind near so as to shoot the duck. They had plenty of vegetables, fish, and game all through the war.

I returned to Richmond and was put in command of a canal barge with five men—captain of a boat with five men at sixteen years of age—to transport 100,000 pounds of stores from Petersburg for the Commissary Department. The boat was narrow and could go through the small passage in the [James River] obstruction at Drewry's Bluff and also through the obstructions in the Appomattox at Fort Clifton. The tug *Banner* would tow us to the obstruction and let go. We poled through, and the tug boat would follow and catch us again and tow down the James and up the Appomattox and leave us at Fort Clifton and return to Richmond and return for us the next day. The tug would not remain in the Appomattox but a few hours for fear the Yankees would come up the James and catch him up there and blockade so as to prevent his return to Richmond. They [the Confederates] could not afford to lose a tug boat. We poled our boat to Petersburg four miles and back when loaded.

Maj. E. B. Branch was quartermaster at Petersburg and had Mr. William S. Finn in his office as clerk. He and the major married sisters, the Misses Lowry. The major is a great Odd Fellow.

The last trip to Petersburg I passed the house [Weston Manor], Sam reported that they caught plenty of fish and were living better. My sister, Mrs. [Sallie] Cake, had a boy, George R. Cake, [born April 30, 1864] who died in 1884, now resting in St. John's churchyard.

We had just fastened up at the [Petersburg] dock when father came up [the Appomattox River in a dugout canoe] and told us the Yankee fleet was in the James River coming up—and our tug had gone to Richmond. Butler's troops landed at Bermuda Hundred about 10 o'clock [on May 5]. Father came up to get some tobacco and said he must hasten home as the Yankees were near their place. I watched him going down the Appomattox with his old blue Yankee overcoat on and felt a presentiment of evil. I never saw him again.

The family got [behind] in the Union lines and about a week later the people moved to Hampton.[51] When they were leaving

51. Many years after the Civil War, George Wood's youngest sister, Emma, recalled the Wood family's harrowing experience of passing through the lines, under the protection of Federal authorities, to return to Hampton. Her account, in part, follows:

> While we were playing at recess, one of the boys looked down the river and saw a fleet of Yankee gunboats coming. The boys mounted their horses and the girls left for home without much ceremony, and the little school house soon looked deserted.
>
> The squadron sailed slowly past City Point and up the river. A portion of the Federal army was stationed at City Point under General Ed-

City Point a Yankee soldier gave Ned a mule, which he took home on Back River.[52]

We waited in Petersburg for orders to come [from the Richmond Quartermaster Department] for about two weeks. We drew our rations and had nothing to do.

---

ward W. Hincks. General Benjamin F. Butler was at Bermuda Hundred. The nearest neighbor was two miles off and we were really between the Federal and Confederate lines.

The next day a squad of Confederate cavalry came in our yard, fired boldly toward the deck of a gunboat passing up the Appomattox and galloped rapidly into the woods. We were so afraid the gunboat would return the fire and we would be killed, so that decided father [to evacuate to Hampton]. He was broken down in health.

My sister, Keturah Pope, taking my brother, Ned, went to City Point and laid our situation before General Hincks. She told him her husband was in the Confederate service and that we had been good rebels but that our brother, Robert Wood, was a strong Union man and had suffered in Libby Prison to atone for any wrong we had done the Union, and in his name we would seek protection.

General Hincks said, "Madam, you and your family will be protected. I will send ambulances with a proper escort to move your family and a physician [Joseph K. Barnes] to accompany your sick sister." Sallie Cake had a little baby two weeks old. The ambulances were soon ready. The soldiers moved on. They advanced slowly but Confederate sharp shooters opened fire and made it too hot to proceed. So they returned in haste.

The next morning the transport, *Lady Lincoln,* under convoy, went to my home. Marines were stationed all around and gunboats ready to open fire on any Confederates that advanced from the wood. My sick sister was tenderly lifted in her chair by the marines and carried aboard the transport, the physician by her side with restoratives if needed. Father and mother with the rest of the family followed and we were soon safe within the Federal lines. On arriving at City Point that afternoon we had served to us the first real coffee and the first "square meal" we had had for six months.

The next day my brother and myself were sent to Bermuda Hundred and in the presence of H. O. Cassell took the Oath of Allegiance to the United States government. We were given passes on the transport *John Warms,* and came to Old Point.

Father remained with his family at City Point until my sister was able

In the meantime General [P. G. T.] Beauregard was having several fights with Butler's forces between Richmond and Petersburg, one came near hemming him in, though Butler had a firm position on a peninsula [Bermuda Hundred between the curls of the James and Appomattox rivers] with gunboats on each side of him and the Confederates with a small force from Lee's army to oppose him.

Grant's army was advancing on Petersburg from City Point. General Grant had crossed his army from Weyanoke on north side to the south side of the James River and was advancing up. He had gotten a head start of General Lee by about two days.

Cullory and myself went to the front to see what was going on. We could see the dust in the distance and occasionally a shell would be thrown over. The Confederates were short of men. Wise's Brigade and city militia was all they had and kept them marching up hill and down to make the enemy believe they were troops coming in when General Lee's army was far away at Cold Harbor and Beauregard could not leave Butler until General Lee's men got up to relieve him.[53]

---

to come to Hampton. They were given free transportation to Old Point and an order to the commanding officer to provide us ambulances to convey us to the home of our brother [William].

We returned to find the town in ruins, my home gone, nothing but a few fruit trees, our two beautiful aspen trees in the front yard and the stone steps were left to what was once the front door.

52. Living at Weston were Robert C. and Susan Wood, their unmarried daughter, Martha, who was called "Mattie" or "Mat"; a three-year-old orphaned grandson, Jefferson Wingfield, who was cared for by Martha; two married daughters, Keturah Pope and Sarah "Sallie" Cake; Sarah's newborn son, George R. Cake; two sons—Sam, eighteen, who, like George, had worked on river transports, and Edward, fifteen, who was called Ned; and their youngest child, Emma Virginia, fourteen.

53. Wise's Brigade was moved on June 9 from the Howlett Line bottling up Butler on Bermuda Hundred to positions along the Dimmock Line east of Petersburg and anchored on the left by the Appomattox River. On the

We got up a mulberry tree to look over the country and eat berries.[54] A shell struck in the field. Someone said: "You better get out of that tree, the enemy think you are observing them from the tree." We just saved ourselves. We got down and went off about fifty yards; another one struck under the tree. We went down again and found the shells were coming over very fast. It was no place for us so we returned to the city [Petersburg].

In about two hours the Confederates were straggling into the city. We asked the news and they answered that the Yankees had taken all our breastworks. It is said by good authority that it was at this time one officer who endeavored to rally his men said to one, "You are behaving like a child." He replied, "I wish I was a child, and a girl child, too."

On that night the Southern troops came over from Beauregard's army and the army wagons and artillery could be heard distinctly. The next afternoon the Confederates charged and took back most of their battery of works lost. The fighting lasted till about 9 o'clock and the moon shone bright, and the rattle of musketry like the sound of wood chopping.

The next morning we expected the Union army to come in to the city. After breakfast I was sitting in the stern of the boat when a gun (32-pound Blakely) from the battery near the bend of the river fired a shell at the railroad bridge that crossed the Appomattox [River] and passed over our heads and struck into a canal barge ahead of us. The barge belonged to Captain South-

---

evening of June 15, Wise's Brigade was attacked and, under an artillery barrage, withdrew. A night attack followed a day later, and bolstered by reinforcements sent from Petersburg by Beauregard, the brigade held. In renewed fighting on June 17, Wise's Brigade fell back, but held as General Lee and the Army of Northern Virginia arrived to establish the defensive works to the east of Petersburg.

54. A berry with a sweet but fairly bland taste that is seldom grown commercially due to its perishable nature.

gate. It struck the top, went through, cut about three feet off the flooring above and three of the bottom timbers and exploded making several holes through the roof. The shot and shell began to go through other houses.

We moved out of the boat and into a brick storehouse. One shell went through the top of an old lady's house at Blandford and through the floor and through the table where she was ironing. She came down on Captain John Foster's sloop, the *Nansemond County,* and told him of the occurrence when one went through the boat awning and buried itself forward.

An old man named Jeter had charge of all the tobacco warehouses. He was deaf and would ask me if the shells were coming. When I saw the puff of smoke [from the cannon], I told him in a short time he would see the explosion. We often ran to where a shell struck, or exploded, and sometimes saw them dug in the ground several feet deep.

One went through the gable end of a colored man's house at Pocahontas when the old man was asleep upstairs. The boys burst through the door to see if he was killed, and he came down growling about people disturbing his sleep. We told him about the shell, he looked at the hole and went back to bed.

One thing I must mention, an old colored teamster was driving a dray through a street [when] a white gentleman dropped down saying, "Oh Lordy," and bowed down when a shell came over. The old darkey stopped the dray and looked back and said, "Why did you call on the Lord now? 'Cause you didn't think of him before?"

One shot struck the bridge [over the Appomattox River]. The engineers had men there to put a prop under it, and while they were there a shell was thrown in the water nearby. Our boats were put in a pontoon bridge so the enemy could not get a good shot at it. (The railroad bridge was a high one.)

That night our boys charged the line and took back some of

the works. It was a beautiful moonlight night and the musketry was fierce. Gen. [William Henry Chase] Whiting attacked the Federals on the north side of the Appomattox River a few days later and gained a great victory, but did not relieve Petersburg.[55]

On that day we went down to see the fight and found General Lee sitting in a shed. Some soldier said, "Keep quiet, there is General Lee." We looked under a shed, and there sat the general with an aide just behind him. I knew him as anyone would recognize him though they had never seen him. It had been two years since I saw him before, and a great change had taken place. He was shorter and older [and looked] like most of the pictures of the present day and not like the young straight soldier.

He was looking at a map, and did not raise his eyes even when a shell burst in front and threw the sand around. We fell flat down, while we were ashamed to look and saw that the general had not noticed it. The staff officers told him a shell had burst in front, and he had better move behind the works as the enemy had the range. He merely said, "Did it?" and moved behind the works.

Passing through the Lines

"Home to Well-Loved Ones"

In June 1864, George Wood was forced to abandon his transport vessel at Petersburg and returned to Richmond to resume running supplies

55. George Wood mistakenly places General Henry Chase Whiting at the fighting in June outside Petersburg. On May 16 at Port Walthall Junction, Whiting, in command of two brigades, allowed two rearguard regiments of Butler's Army of James to withdraw unopposed to safety behind Federal lines on Bermuda Hundred. The timid commander, at his own request, was relieved of command.

on the James River to Confederate defensive positions downstream. After he learned of his father's death, he decided to return to Hampton to be with his mother. With Cullory, he slipped through Confederate lines and surrendered to Federal authorities. He took the oath of allegiance and at City Point was given passage for Hampton.

We had nothing to do as the boats were taken from us. We reported to Richmond and found that the quartermaster at Petersburg had neglected to inform our quartermaster that we were idle in Petersburg. He thought we were being used on the Appomattox [River].

I was put in a new boat to run stores to Drewry's and Chaffin's bluffs. While there heard of the death of my father [in Hampton on June 7, 1864], and I resolved at first opportunity to come home to mother.

A few days before I left I was taken up by the city patrols that got every man they could pick up to go to the front. We had a certificate from Major Harvey, quartermaster, saying I was under age, but I was liable to go in the reserves, which was from sixteen to eighteen, but Captain Coke, the conscript officer, said I was doing more good in the Quartermaster Department than I could in the field and if taken would have to be detailed to do the same work. We often heard that the South was robbing the cradle and the grave for their army and this referred to the late order taking from sixteen to eighteen and forty-five to fifty years all in the reserve corps.

Captain Cullory, who ran one of the boats, would go down [the James River] one day while my boat was loading and I would go down the next day with the supplies for the Commissary Department. When he was in Richmond he thought of going north to Brooklyn, New York, as he was tired, he said, of the war.

He made his intentions known to the old colored man on

lower Main Street who ran a blacksmith shop. He was a yellow man. He said he could get him a guide for $200. He [Cullory] then asked me to join him, and I consented. We provided knapsacks, and the *Banner* took down my boat that morning about 7 o'clock and I told Captain Trower I wanted to stop in the city all day.

We passed down Main Street through Rockets on the morning of the 18th of October 1864, purchased loaf bread and bologna sausage, and the *Enquirer* and *Examiner,* two of the daily papers published in Richmond, kept down the York River Rail Road track, passed the Chimborazo Hospital and looking ahead for the guide who came out from under the trees with his gun on his shoulder.

I knew the man well and I knew I could trust him, but he did right in trusting no one. His name was Benj. Wood. (No relation of Hampton Woods.) He said nothing, but beckoned us to follow him. He kept down the road about three miles, turned to the right and went through a skirt of woods, halted, motioned to us to do the same.

A horseman rode up the road. A motion to come across the road to another woods, through it about one mile, halt, and we joined the guide. "Wait here," said he, "until I find the pickets."

The weather was warm; a thunder cloud was gathering. We sat down and ate our dinner as it was 11½ o'clock. We waited an hour and no guide returned. We were uneasy, afraid of being captured and taken back to Richmond and perhaps to Libby Prison. We pushed along through the wood. The rain poured down. We clung close to the trees. We had on blue Yankee overcoats that we had purchased from some colored person who picked them up after being thrown away by the Union soldiers. The rain lasted about half hour when it ceased. We were wet and started through wood to look for the Union pickets. We got to an opening with a house in the center of the field and an apple orchard in the field. We could see no one, and began to gather apples. Cullory hastened across the field and over the fence and across the road running east and west. He saw a man in the house at a distance which caused him to run.

I followed, getting in a skirt of woods, again with a road on each side running north and south. Cullory went to the right and saw a picket on horseback and ran back to the left.

I remarked, "We are near that other road," when someone said, "Who comes dere?"

We had to answer "friend," and went out to the troops on horseback. We were not shown what army he belonged to because many Southern soldiers wore blue coats when hard up for overcoats.

We were encouraged by his broken English as there were few foreigners in our army.

He asked, "Ver you go?"

Cullory replied, "Toward the river."

"You can't go dat vay," he said.

"Do you belong to the Union army?" I asked.

He said he did, to the Pennsylvania cavalry.

I said, "You are the man we are looking for [since] we left Richmond this morning and have been looking for you all day," and took a seat on the grass.

The trooper said, "Vait till de officers comes around."

When the captain came up, the trooper said, "Here ish two men what gifs themselfs up."

"Where did you come from, boys?" said captain.

"Richmond," I replied.

"Are you sure?" said he.

"Yes," we answered, "Here is the *Enquirer* of today."

He looked at it and was sure of that fact. "Where did you get your overcoats?"

And we explained where we got them.

"Are you native Virginians?" he asked.

We answered "yes," one born in Augusta County and the other in Elizabeth City County.

He thought we were Northern men, but we had our papers to show we were employed in the Confederate Quartermaster Department and not soldiers and wanted to go to Hampton and New York. We were well treated, given a drink out of his canteen, introduced to the major, who was a German.

He said, "Dat schwein vas crazy as he wanted to hang me ven I vas prisoner."

Was given in charge of a trooper to be conducted to Butler's headquarters at Varina, or, we called it, Aiken's Landing. The trooper trusted us and rode off some distance to find the way to the headquarters, which showed that he trusted us.

We got in the pen at Butler's headquarters with a log fire in the center. It was cold, damp ground, and we were tired and slept until toward morning and chilled when awakened. This was the first night during the war that I had slept on the ground. I kept stirring around until I got warm. About 8 o'clock we had breakfast of hot coffee in a pint tin cup, about the second cup of coffee for two years, a piece of pork and hardtack, and after getting this breakfast was comfortable.

A missionary passed through the prison pen and from him got paper, stamps, and envelope and wrote to [George's brother] S. B. Wood at Old Point, which he got next day, and all the family rejoiced.

I recognized Tom Massenburg as one of the prisoners for exchange. Tom said he was in the secret or spy service and was captured near Smithfield. A party of these men would board vessels at night on the James River, take all the valuables and set fire to the vessel. This caused the Union authorities to land men at Smithfield, and Tom was captured. Tom said he had to go to work in the [Dutch Gap] canal to keep the Confederates from firing on the men who were digging there [at Dutch Gap].

Albert Aiken's place is about two miles below Dutch Gap and was called Varina by the Federals and was used as a place of exchange for prisoners in 1862 and '63. The Union forces had a pontoon bridge across here, and the monitors and fleet were anchored below the bridge. They could cross on this bridge and march over to a neck of land to Bermuda Hundred in about two hours, while it was twenty-five miles around by steamer on account of the winding of the river (or five miles across land).

Lieutenant Donovan of General Butler's staff questioned me, but I could not give him any news from the South, but told him that the South had to depend on the Danville Railroad for supplies from the south.

We were taken in charge by half-dozen troopers and marched that afternoon and evening [across the pontoon bridge over the James] to Bermuda Hundred. The moon shone beautiful and all were happy as they were going home to well-loved ones. The troopers were kind and would stop when anyone was tired. There were about two hundred in our party. We arrived at Bermuda Hundred at 8 o'clock and were drawn up in a line before Lt. James Noyes, assistant provost marshal, and took the oath. When I signed, he asked if I was related to Billy Wood of Hampton.

We slept cramped up in an old house, which I recognized as one occupied two years back by Mr. Crawford, Dr. Eppes' overseer of Eppes Island, just opposite of the hundreds. The next morning we were on steamers to City Point just across the mouth of the Appomattox River. We had a building and yard enclosed by a high fence. The Yankees had erected a large building in an open lot, and Grant's log house headquarters was about three-hundred yards north of us. I would go sometimes

"Rendezvous of Our [Federal] Fleet in James River, off City Point" in 1862, from *Harper's Magazine,* June 21, 1862, p. 390. (Special Collections, University of Virginia)

down the hill to the Appomattox River to get water in a barrel. The barrel had two hand-pieces nailed to side for handles. A man in front and one in rear to carry it down this hill, which was where we had our fish fry in 1861.

I would look over and see many places where I had played in 1861: the little Methodist church where we would hear the queer preacher on the order of Samuel Jones, and the Episcopal churchyard where sister Elizabeth Wingfield and niece Mollie Pope laid buried.

In about seven days we got on board the fast steamer *New York* and passed swiftly down the river, passing Jordan's Point, Harrison's Landing, Berkeley, Westover, Ruffin's, Wilcox, Fort Powhatan, Claremont, Jamestown, and just at sunset passed Newport's News, as we always called it (or Nephus News); now it is called Newport News. It was a camping ground for a regi-

ment of men [Camp Butler] where it once was, before the war, a store kept by Merriam and Gill. Mr. Hawkins and Mr. Parrish had houses there.

Returning to Hampton

"I Once More Gazed on God's Land"

George Wood was greeted on his return by his brother Sam, but he was detained by Federal authorities. His sister Keturah Pope and brother Ned secured a pass for him to visit his mother, who had resettled on the Back River because the family home in Pee Dee had been torn down by Federal soldiers. George found Hampton crowded with contrabands living in slab houses and convalescent Confederate soldiers wandering about. Despite the devastation, some merchants had re-

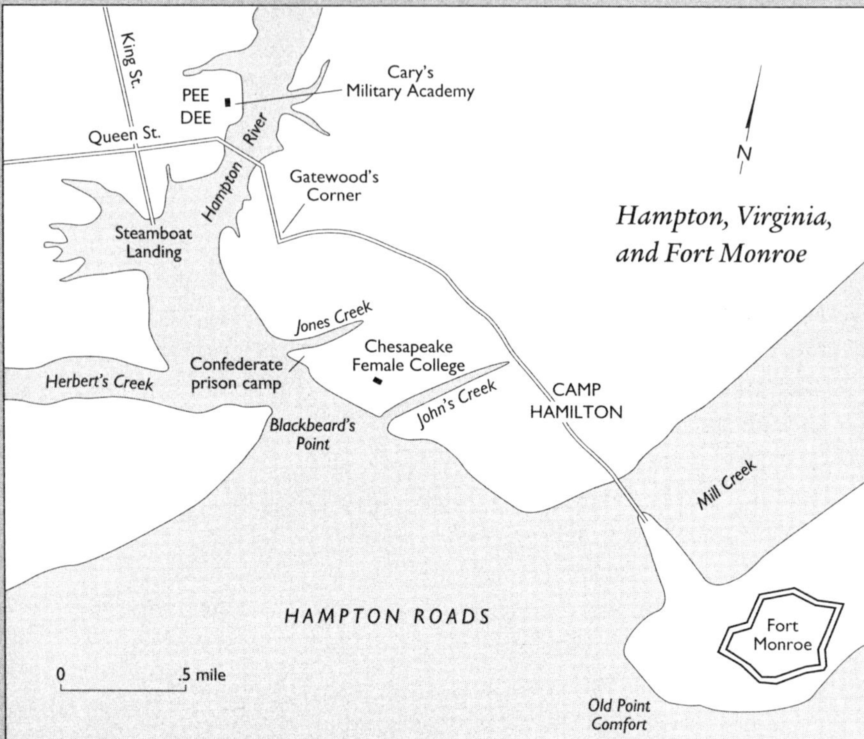
Hampton, Virginia, and Fort Monroe
King St.
Queen St.
PEE DEE
Cary's Military Academy
Hampton River
Gatewood's Corner
Steamboat Landing
N
Jones Creek
Chesapeake Female College
Confederate prison camp
Herbert's Creek
John's Creek
CAMP HAMILTON
Blackbeard's Point
Mill Creek
HAMPTON ROADS
Fort Monroe
0
.5 mile
Old Point Comfort

turned and farmers and watermen were doing brisk business. Later, George helped his older brothers John (Jack) and William (Billy) build a home for their mother.

When the ship turned into Hampton Roads I once more gazed on God's land as the Israelites looked over to the Promised Land. So I gazed at the fort, Rip Raps, Chesapeake Female College, and the ruins of Hampton that I had not seen for four [*sic*] long years, and inhaled the salt breezes from the east wind off the old ocean.

We landed at a new wharf [Baltimore Wharf at Fort Monroe], one built during the war and the one now used at this time. Before the war steamers landed at the lighthouse wharf [Engineer Wharf]. The place [immediately outside the fort's moat] that only had half-dozen houses before the war now had a small village. Kimberly had a ship store; Bentley, a jewelry store. The large Hygeia Hotel had been torn down. There were in half-moon shops opposite the Sherwood House storing houses for army stores of all kind such as forage, clothing, tents, mattresses, &c. that lined the road.

Sam was there to meet me and told me the folks were ready to receive me as one from the dead. He got me some cheese and crackers as he knew I had not eaten any cheese for four years. Cheese could not be easily gotten in the South. He had an old fashioned nine-pence piece he kept through the war to buy some cheese when he got home.

We marched from there to Camp Hamilton, or Camp Distribution[56] at the old Chesapeake Female College ground, now the Soldiers Home. We went by a then-new road around through Roseland, then Mr. Joe Segar's place, now Mrs. [Harrison] Phoe-

56. So named because there soldiers were taken and drilled and distributed to work in farm fields.

bus' place. All along the route were stone houses—mess house for employees to live in and wagon-building shops—until we arrived at the Bull Pen, as it was called. It was erected on a V-shaped point of land with Hampton River on one side and College [Jones] Creek on the other. Captain Blake of the 5th Pennsylvania heavy artillery was in the commander's quarters, in the old house at the large willow tree.

A high board fence with heavy wooden gates ran across the head of the prison and the other part was surrounded by water [and there] was a walkway for guards. The only house there was a long building for men to sleep in. One of Hampton's well-known citizens who was confined in this prison made his escape one dark, stormy night by digging under the fence and swimming across the creek.

The original college building was used as a hospital and dispensary, and the house was occupied by the Rev. Charles A. Raymond, Baptist minister, former principal of the college, afterwards governor of the home, and one other small building.

Captain Putnam, with two companies of U.S. infantry, occupied this camp for about two years after the war closed, as a police station before the state reentered the Union. In the building used as headquarters was where I remembered as having passed part of a Sunday about six years before during a thunderstorm, having disobeyed my mother and went there after Sabbath school to get mulberries from the larger tree there then, and took the storm as a visitation for my disobediences.

Next morning we got into line and marched up, received our breakfast consisting of a ten-pint can of coffee, pieces of boiled pork, several hardtack or large crackers, and ate it with a good relish. My name was called by the sergeant and told I was wanted at the captain's office. It reminded me of the old saying on the James River steamboats when the porters (darkies) would go round the steamer with a handbill saying or singing: "All who have not settled dese fare will walk to de capen's office and settle it dare."

But I was not very uneasy because I had done nothing and had good Union friends outside who would see me out. I found my sister, Mrs. [Keturah] Pope, and Ned in a mule cart with a pass for twenty-four hours to go home. When our people left City Point, a soldier said to Ned, "Sonny, don't you want a mule to work your farm with when you get home," and Ned took the mule and brought it home. The mule had been captured by some raiding party.

Our people lived on Back River at the Horn place, now Charles Latimore's. Our two houses had not been burnt, but were torn down by the 6th Maine Regiment to make plank floors for their tents. When we went there, there was nothing but a pile of bricks from the chimney and the two aspen trees at the riverbank. My work in the [Confederate] Quartermaster Department netted me $140. Ned sold his mule for $100, and Sam got the claim we had against [a man named] Parkerson before the war of $90, and with these amounts we [at a later time] put up a building to live in on the Pee Dee lot. I assisted Jack, who did the carpentry work, while Billy did the brick work.

We had to pass through Hampton, and I noticed a [horse]car line running from Gatewood's Corner across the College Creek at the now Empire House, around the rear of the main building, out a northeast course across John's Creek, straight down through Ruben Clark's place. Near the bridge was a store in Colonel Tabb's house. This was once a summer hotel and in all the buildings Tabb and Whitings were together; next was a sentinel house and sentry on duty at east side of Hampton Bridge where you had to show your pass. On the west side of the creek on the right-hand where once was the elegant residence of Dr. Vaughan's and Hampton Military Academy, with its fine

Drawing of the ruins of Hampton, Virginia, by Richardson, showing Queen Street bridge across the Hampton River looking westward toward Pee Dee. (Virginia Historical Society, 1999.161.449)

building and beautiful lawns, were Negro slab houses, dirt chimneys, and corn growing in many places where once was beautiful lawns, and it was the same with many other places.

Mrs. Garrett's, Captain Anderson's, Dr. Semple's, all owned brick residences that were destroyed, and huts were there. The walls of St. John's Church, Court House, and Mr. K[ennon] Whiting's house were left standing, and the woodwork destroyed.

Mr. Samuel Cumming had built and reestablished his business, a general store. He was the first to build in December 1862. Captain Tennis was in business at the ferry shore. Samuel Thanhouser, a Baltimore man, was in dry goods and grocery business. A Freedman's store was where Darden's store is now. Dr. Hull was in the drug business, and a few small shops were doing business in town.

There were hundreds of colored contrabands, as the Negroes were called, on the streets, and no one dared to say anything against them or he would be called an "old white secesh." Negroes had come here from all parts of the state wherever the Union army had been and remained here for protection, and many had obtained work in the different departments and had settled on the abandoned lots and farms. They built slab houses made out of the abandoned wood and made chimneys with sticks piled up and with the cracks filled with clay. One settlement on Mill Creek was called Slab Town. On Mill Creek near Mr. Kelly's property was a large field where the Federals had a cattle corral.

Money was plentiful as there were thousands of soldiers in hospitals. Extending from Gatewood's Corner, all on the right-hand side to Butler's School and Soldiers Home, long buildings, yellow washed. Many convalescent soldiers would be roaming around.

Besides the immense amount of government work, the oysters on the rocks had grown in four years and were plentiful and a tonger could make $10 a day.

All the neighboring farmers had a good trade with milk, vegetables, chickens, and eggs, &c, but none of them seemed to have saved their money, and the merchants got broke after the war.

The War Ends

"All Went on a Spree"

While detained, George Wood was weary of unsavory inmates and cast a vote for Abraham Lincoln in an apparent mock presidential election. By the end of November 1864 he was released and found work in a blacksmith shop—and an unexpected disturbance at a magic lantern show. The news on April 3, 1865, that Richmond had fallen was celebrated with fireworks at Fort Monroe and with despair by impoverished white citizens in Hampton.

We remained in prison at Camp Hamilton owing to the St. Albans raiders [October 19, 1864]. It was reported that Southern people were deserting to destroy northern property. In our prison were a lot of deserters (Union) or bounty jumpers who would rob (mug they called it) every man who had money who came into the prison. They did it by throwing a blanket over the head of the victim and held his arms while the others went through his pockets. If you said anything, they were abused, and many wished themselves back in the Confederacy.

We had a polling precinct opened November 7 to see how the camp stood for Lincoln or McClellan. I voted for Lincoln because I had no confidence in McClellan either as a general or statesman. It was said it was only in fun, but perhaps the vote was counted.

We got out at the end of three weeks with a pass from Captain Meyers, provost marshal, [and I] went home. I have never heard from my friend [Cullory], who went to New York. After spending two weeks at home visiting friends, I went to work in W. H. Frinick's blacksmith's shop [in what is now] Phoebus on the Soldiers Home Road, helping with a man named Reid from Petersburg. He was a Scotchman but had come through the lines from Petersburg. He was a Mason and Odd Fellow, and those men—Masons and Odd Fellows—could get almost any favor during the war. We worked pleasantly together for four months.

All men had a nickname. Mine was Long Tom because I was so tall [six feet, two inches]. Noah Pike was called Yank because he was from Maine state. Charles Shannon, an Irishman, was caterer of our mess.[57] We lived in a long building called a mess house with eating tables at the end and a passage running through the other part with rooms on each side.

We could see a large body of men march from Camp Distribution past our shops daily going to the front and [at Petersburg] Grant was massing his troops around Lee.

I was working there when Greble Lodge [Number 137 of the Independent Order of Odd Fellows] was established, and many of the boys joined, but I was only 17 years old and could not join.[58]

I was sick for one week and kindly attended by Dr. Seymour, who was allowed to attend to citizens. The chief surgeon was Dr. McCleland, who occupied Colonel Mallory's house.

57. A group of men who regularly prepare and eat their meals together.

58. George Wood, who became a member of the secret, fraternal, and benefit society on April 25, 1869, notes elsewhere in his journal that the Greble Lodge, named in honor of Union Lieutenant John T. Greble, killed at the Battle of Big Bethel, was "instituted" February 2, 1865, at Fort Monroe and "came under the jurisdiction of the Grand Lodge of Virginia in 1866 and moved to Hampton." Initially, lodge members met in an "upper room" of a grist mill on Hope Street that was owned by J. S. Darling. Sometime in the 1870s a lodge hall was erected on Queen Street.

One night we went to a magic lantern show in a schoolhouse where Larrabee lives. It was conducted by a mulatto from Cuba. Moses Reddick had an apple and peanut stand in one corner of the room. The place was filled with convalescent soldiers.

The exhibitor said, "Gentlemens, I'll show de picter of down souf whar de white folks left de plantation to de care of the colored folks. All dat can sing will sing and dance. What can't sing will shut up deis moufs."

When he produced the picture, everyone [began] howling in a different tune. Men made [shadow] pictures on the curtain with [their] fingers. The apple stand was turned over, apples were thrown about the room, lights were put out and bricks thrown in the window. The men went out, made the man give back their money. In fact, the man paid out more than he took in as many said they had expected to go in who had not been in at all. I found out that the Yankees did not love the colored people as much as our Southern people.

At 11 o'clock [Monday, April 3, 1865] we got news of the capture of Richmond.[59] Mr. Reid threw away his apron and went to Old Point. The whistles on all the steamers in the harbor began to blow and bells commenced to ring. The boss gave half-day holiday and all went on a spree. At night a grand display of fireworks were had at the fort.

Work gradually ceased in all the departments shops. Hospital wards were sold and pulled down.[60] Our people began to return in deep distress to commence life anew, the larger portion with nothing to commence with—many with debts hanging over their property, some with property confiscated, and

59. Richmond Mayor Joseph Mayo surrendered the city early in the morning of April 3, 1865, as the last Confederate soldiers and government officials crossed over the James River.

60. One of these rough structures was moved to North King Street and used temporarily as a Methodist Church.

breakfast consisting of a tin Pt Cup of Coffee piece Of Mess Pork boiled several hard tacks or larger and ate it with a good relish. My name was Called by the Sergent and told I was wanted at Captains Office it reminded me of the old saying on the James River Steam boats when the Porter darky Would go around the Steamer with a hand bell saying or Sing

All who have not settled dere fare Will walk to de Capens office and settle it dare but I was not very uneasy because I had done Nothing and had good union friends out side Who would see me out. I found my Sister Mrs P... and Ned in a Mule Cart with a pass for 24 hours to go home. When our people left City point a Soldier Said to Ned Sonny dont you want a Mule to work your farm with when you get home and Ned took the Mule [belongs to him] that had been Captured by some raiding party. Our people lived at the Ham place now Chas Tat... We had to pass through Hampton and I noticed a Car line running from Gatewoods Corner across the College Creek to the now Engine House around the rear of the ... buildings out a N. East Course across Johns Creek Straight a... through Ruben Clarks place – near the bridge was a Store in Col. Labbs House – this was once a ... Hotel and all the buildings Labbs and Whitings were ... next was a Sentinal house and Sentry on duty at east side Hampton bridge where you had to show your pass. – on the West side of the Creek on the right hand where once was The elegant residence of Dr Vaughan Hampton Military academy with its fine building and beautiful lawns were negro Slab Houses dirt Chimneys and Corn growing ...

some others with property in possession of the contrabands, who refused to give it up, and required a military force to dispossess them of it.

One of the old citizens, quite wealthy before the war, came down from Richmond, and his hat blew off. He came by the shop bareheaded. A fellow remarked, "Four years in the Confederacy and come home bareheaded, which expresses our poverty."

Robert B. Wood

"He Was a Union Man"

The wartime experiences of his brother, imprisoned because he retained an allegiance to the Union, were of special interest to George Wood, who, along with all other members of the family, always defended Robert B. Wood. After the Civil War, the community accepted him as an esteemed citizen. In reporting his death in 1898, the *Daily Press* called him "a gentleman of fine character," and said that his funeral was "notable for the large attendance of elderly people."

When I got home I visited [my brother] R[obert] B. Wood, who lived at Samuel Phillips' place on Hampton Creek. I got him to relate his experiences during the war.

When Hampton was evacuated he went to William Phillips, his father-in-law's place, on Back River. One night in August [1861] the house was surrounded by Southern men and he [was] captured and carried to Yorktown and thence to Richmond via West Point. They examined him and found no charge except he was a Union man and would not take the oath to the Confederacy, so he was put in the old Richmond jail.[61]

61. Despite George's protestations of his brother's innocence of spying, Ann M. Hopkins gave a sworn deposition on September 2, 1861, that she saw

In the jail were two men, [John] Scully and his companion whose name I have forgotten [Price Lewis], who were in the Secret Service under Col. [Allan] Pinkerton. These men were sent there [to Richmond] to find what was the matter with Capt. [Timothy] Webster, who was one of their men and was laid up with rheumatism. The letter from Baltimore was found and caused suspicion against these men who were jailed, and Webster was finally hanged. (A full account of this escape and recapture can be found in Pinkerton's war stories.[62])

These men [Scully and Lewis] were eager to escape so they would not have to appear against Webster. They had an old wrench [with] which they took the bolts off the doors or out of the locks, replacing them with wooden bolts smearing white-wash over the evidence. The door was a heavy oaken one butting so tight that a knife blade could not be got in to open it as it swung shut.

---

a map drawn by Robert B. Wood of the Fox Hill neighborhood "with all the roads and houses of prominent citizens marked on it" and that she heard Wood say "he intended to give it to the Federal troops." And Lieutenant Richard M. Booker of Elizabeth City County testified on October 8, 1861, that when he was home on leave "sometime in June," he was told that "Mr. Robert Wood had furnished a map of the country to the enemy."

The 1860 census records an Ann M. Hopkins, fifteen, living with the family of Francis W. Guy, thirty-one, a harbor pilot with real estate estimated to be worth $12,500, and his wife, Sallie A. Guy, and their three children—Alice, five; Frank, three; and a one-month-old infant. Also living in the household was Thomas Ash, nineteen, an apprentice to become a pilot. The Guy family resided in the same neighborhood as Robert B. Wood and his family.

George's sister, Emma, claims in her unpublished "Notes on the Civil War" that their brother Robert "was arrested through the false accusation of Mrs. Frank Brittingham and Captain Frank Guy, Sr."

62. *The Spy of the Rebellion,* published by G.W. Carleton and Company in 1883.

A prisoner had to be concealed outside to shove the door open. [When] they went in the yard to chop up their wood for the night, the jailor stood at a distance, and the smallest man was covered over in the ashes with a piece of old stove pipe near his mouth, the straw sprinkled over the ashes to hide the fresh appearance. They went in and rigged a dummy in the man's bed to account for the prisoner outside. When the jailor made his rounds, one of the other men in the room answered for him, saying he had hurt his back and was asleep.

Next to the jail was a tobacco factory, and somehow the Negroes knew they were to attempt an escape and sang the songs as they were accustomed to do very loud. About 11 o'clock they began, and in half an hour out of the jail they made for the Chickahominy and thence across to the Rappahannock with rain pouring down. After traveling about two days starved [and] weary, asked for food, and the man who they asked for bread gave them a stone, or put the home guard on them, brought them back to Richmond.[63]

He [Robert B. Wood] and some of his companions with spoons tunneled under the prison walls, hiding the dirt under

63. George Wood doesn't say specifically that his brother was among the prisoners who broke out of the Henrico Jail with Scully and Lewis on the night of March 18, 1862. His recitation of their escape and capture closely parallels Pinkerton's account of the episode in chapter 35 of his book. Scully and Lewis, who were British subjects working as Pinkerton detectives, had been sent to check on Timothy Webster, a Union agent then ill in his Richmond hotel room, when they were identified as spies and put in the county jail.

After their jailbreak, capture, and return to jail, Scully and Lewis revealed to Confederate authorities—perhaps unintentionally—Webster's role in carrying Confederate mail between Richmond and Baltimore so it could be intercepted and read by Union agents. Webster was summarily tried and hung as a spy. Scully and Lewis were paroled North.

the beds, and in the spring of 1862 they were to attempt their escape when McClellan's army got near Richmond.[64]

The morning before the night they were to attempt their escape they were moved to Salisbury, N.C. After the prisoners got to Salisbury they read in a Richmond paper a few weeks later an article headed: "The Jail Birds About To Fly Again." They [the Richmond prison guards] had found the tunnel or excavation.

They made another tunnel in Salisbury and sent one man to get bread, and he was followed back because he bought such a quantity. They were brought back to Richmond. His people often sent him food while in Richmond prisons—Libby and

64. A Confederate commissioner, S. S. Baxter, interrogated Robert B. Wood after his failed jailbreak. Baxter's April 26, 1862, report reads, in part:

> On the 13th or 14th of June, he says (he met) three or four men who said they were deserters [apparently from Fort Monroe] and wanted to go to the Southern army. Some days after that he was walking around his father-in-law's plantation. Some of the Federal soldiers took him prisoner and carried him to Fortress Monroe and he was released on parole. A few nights afterwards a party came to the house of his father-in-law, took all the men there except himself; took them to the fort and made them take the oath. He thinks they knew he had been at the fort and, therefore, they did not take him. He solemnly declares this was all the communication he had with the enemy. When Miss [Ann M.] Hopkins' affidavit was shown him he admitted he had been to Topping's after a Negro belonging to his father-in-law. He first admitted he saw the Northern troops, but afterward said they were leaving when he got there and he saw them at a distance and did not converse with them. He got the Negro and denies the truth of all the other statements made by Miss Hopkins. I return Miss Hopkins' desposition. Denies he had any pass except permission to pass the pickets when he was discharged from imprisonment at Fortress Monroe. Denies he had ever promised to make a map and denies he ever did make a map. I think this man's manner under examination was very bad. He was confused and obviously attempting to suppress the truth. He is one of the party who broke jail, and in relation to that matter he prevaricated very much. If evidence can be procured he ought to be brought to trial as a spy.

Castle Thunder—or he might have fared worse. As it was he was white as paper and came near dying at prison [before] he was exchanged—in all making nineteen months in prison.

He got well and [after the Civil War] filled many offices of trust nearly until his death in 1898. He was collector of internal revenue for twenty years, postmaster about three years.

Epilogue

Even though Hampton was not a battlefield, "the strife of war," George Wood observed, "despoiled this old town of its former beauty." Sadly and realistically, he predicted "long years must yet elapse before it will regain its picturesque attractiveness of days of yore."

Yet he and his brothers didn't pause to bemoan their family's loss. Their parents' home in the Pee Dee neighborhood might be "nothing but a pile of bricks from the chimney," but John, a carpenter by trade, and Billy, a brick mason, and Sam and George, a pair of handymen, pooled their financial resources—$330 all counted—and "put up a house [for their widowed mother] on the old place and," as George wrote in his journal, "began life again."

So, too, did their neighbors as they returned to restore their lives, their homesteads, and their community.

The federal government sold the wooden hospital wards erected on the grounds of the Chesapeake Female College, and residents salvaged the boards and hardware. Others moved entire buildings and adopted them for housing. One of the wards was put up on North King Street and used as a temporary Methodist church.

In his journal, Wood noted that the prominent carpenters at that time of Reconstruction were J. W. Brown, an undertaker; Charles Davis Cake, his brother-in-law; John Wood, his brother; and W. T. Daougherty, H. D. Owens, and R. S. Hosier.

General Benjamin Butler bought the Chesapeake Female College in 1867 and the next year sold it to the U.S. government for use as a home for aging Union veterans, which opened in

1870. At one time—Wood doesn't say exactly when—there were "about 3,300 of the old boys in the house." The institution was "fitted up with all the modern improvements, beautiful trees, flowers, lawns, and walks"—and a superb view of "the passing steamers and vessels from Richmond, Newport News, Norfolk, Baltimore, Washington, and from the ocean besides."

The Soldiers Home adjoined the Hampton Agricultural and Normal Institute, established in 1868 under the leadership of Samuel Chapman Armstrong, a Northern general. The site, Wood recalled, once "belonged to the Drummond family and at one time had a wind grist mill on it." Prior to the Civil War it was owned by Dr. William E. Wood [no relation], who sold a portion of his property in 1867 for a National Cemetery.

Hampton Academy was rebuilt on Pee Dee Point in 1870.

George Wood's uncle, Samuel W. Wood, who had served as a pilot aboard the CSS *Fredericksburg*, borrowed money and built a pilot boat, which he named *Phantom*. A man of proven political savvy, Samuel Wood organized the Virginia Pilots Association in 1866 and served as its first president. By then, the harbor pilots of Hampton Roads had transferred their base to Norfolk.

Elizabeth City County Court was reestablished in 1870 with Judge W. R. Willis, formerly an officer in the Thirty-second Virginia Regiment, presiding. Among the attorneys George Wood listed are men named Tabb, Mallory, Peek, Willis, and Hughes. Wood did not give their full names, but added, "S. W. Armistead and A. S. Segar afterwards became lawyers."

Among the physicians who resumed practice were "Doctors Semple, Jennings, and Hope." Wood notes that "Dr. Seymour, a Northern physician, was established when the other doctors came home." In 1870, a "Dr. Shield was added to the corps of physicians," and doctors James T. Boutelle and Charles Selden "were added" in 1874, followed by Jesse H. Peek in 1878 and Walter Plecker in 1890.

Wood reported that a Freedman's store was established in 1865 with Harry Bersh as manager, but that it "failed."

An example of postwar hard times is evident in this stark journal entry: "J. A. Parker became the mail carrier to Old Point, down at night and up in the morning. His horse died and then he carried it on his back for two years."

Wood offered somewhat of a disjointed directory of the business community that emerged after the war:

"Dr. [Henry] Hull kept a drug store. Afterward McDevitt & Wood [his brother, Sam] opened a dry store on the corner King and Queen. Henry Lancer kept a beer garden on Queen Street."

Back from serving the Confederacy, Marion Colbert opened a book store; Francis Anton Schmelz returned to his bakery.

Among the grocers, who also dispensed liquor, were H. C. Whiting, T. W. Roche, and George's brother-in-law, J. W. Richardson. Titlow and Hefflefinger opened a lumber and coal yard; Sheetz and Tunic opened a blacksmith and wheelwright shop.

George Wood added to his summary:

"Mr. John S. Moody established a large department store, drugs, dry goods, grocery, hardware, but it did not succeed.

"J. J. Barnes established the Kecoughtan Hotel south on King Street.

"Tennis & Co. moved on West Queen Street from east side of [Hampton] river. [J. H.] Gosline moved his marine railway to west side from east side [of the river].

"J. S. Darling and Blevin erected a plane mill on Hope Street and rented the upper room to Greble Lodge that was established at Old Point, but moved to Hampton in 1866.

"The Masons were notified from the Baltimore lodge that their jewels and other lodge property were held for them, and the lodge resumed labor in 1867, and met at Greble Hall on Hope Street."

Hampton Agricultural and Normal Institute (the predecessor of Hampton University), which was established in 1868 by U.S. General Samuel Chapman Armstrong, "began to receive Northern aid," and as Wood reported, "many new buildings were added."

Wood gave scant attention to the men from the North associated with Hampton's seafood industry that flourished for almost a century after the Civil War—James McMenamin, Charles E. Hewins, J. E. Robinson, and J. S. Darling.

Almost in passing, Wood referred to the extension of the Chesapeake and Ohio (C&O) Railway from Newport News to Old Point in 1882, a curious oversight since Hampton businessmen petitioned Collis P. Huntington to build the railroad to Newport News.

In 1870, George Wood was still working as a blacksmith at Fort Monroe and living with his mother, Susan Hicks Wood; his oldest sister, Mattie, who told the census taker her occupation was that of a milliner; his brother, Ned, a "ship carpenter"; his youngest sister, Emma, a teenage milliner; and his nephew, "Jessie" Wingfield, a school boy.

On the day after Christmas 1872, Susan Hicks Wood died, and sometime within the next few years Ned married. Emma married John Wesley Richardson in 1876. Jeff Wingfield also left the household when he married, leaving George and Mattie to share the house.

Until 1875, George Wood worked as a clerk at Bickford's general store outside Fort Monroe on Old Point Comfort and then for several other shopkeepers, the last being his brother, Sam. After that he went to work for Harrison Phoebus at the Hygeia Hotel on Old Point Comfort, at various times serving as night clerk, cashier, and express driver. "During that time," Wood wrote with a hint of intrigue, "Mr. Phoebus was the best of friends, but he had people around him who controlled him and he afterwards saw his error in not promoting me, so I left."

Subsequently he once again clerked for his brother Sam and other store owners.

In 1877, Sam Wood organized a voluntary military unit, the Peninsula Guards. It was an outgrowth of a popular baseball team and was composed of prominent men in Hampton who acquired their own uniforms and paraded on Confederate Memorial Day and at other public events. For more than two decades Sam served as captain of the Guards, which became Company D of the Fourth Virginia Regiment of Volunteers and was mobilized for the Spanish-American War. George Wood held the elected post of fourth sergeant when the Peninsula Guards were formed, but it is unknown how long he remained an active participant.

On February 1, 1878, George Wood entered into a business relationship with Henry Clay Whiting, a Confederate veteran fifteen years his senior, who at that time opened a grocery and drug store in the first block of West Queen Street.

In 1881, Wood—to use his phrase—"took up the drug department" in Whiting's store. Five years later he was a licensed pharmacist, the first in Hampton. When Whiting died in 1899, Wood took over the business. In a back room of the drug store there was a private drinking club restricted to Confederate veterans. The password to enter was "Boot, boot."

George Wood was the Hampton correspondent for the *Soldiers Home Bulletin,* a weekly newspaper that began publication in December 1884 and had a wide general circulation. Occasionally his articles were signed "George Randolph." Since copies of the *Bulletin* survive, Wood's columns amount to a lively—and opinionated—history of Hampton through November 1891 when, Wood explained, "all the staff had other work to attend to."

The *Home Bulletin* allowed Wood to pontificate on local affairs and promote the economic development of Hampton. "We advocated and called attention to many matters which were established," Wood wrote in his journal. "First, the incorporation of Hampton with its lights and police, the building of the railroad and an iron bridge [for it]. We called attention of bridge builders [improving the Queen Street Bridge] to the necessity of providing a walkway across so people's lives would not be endangered by runaway horses."

His account of a fire that mysteriously broke out in April 1887 at the home of his business partner, H. C. Whiting, a widower at the time, serves as an apt example of his folksy style of news reporting—and his fondness for using commas:

> Between half past two and three o'clock, Tuesday morning, a fire broke out in the smoke house of Mr. H. C. Whiting, near the bridge, and it soon spread to the hen house, and from thence to the kitchen, attached to the main dwelling house. Mr. Whiting, and his daughter, Miss Jennie, were the only occupants of the house at the time, save a lady visitor and two female servants. Mr. Whiting manned the pump, while Miss Jennie mounted the kitchen roof, and, as the water was passed to her, bravely fought the fiery element, and prevented the dwelling from catching on fire, until succor arrived from Hampton, in the persons of Policeman Watson and several young men who were just going home from the Hop, and discovered the fire after it had been burning fifteen or twenty minutes. By their aid the flames were prevented from spreading any farther, and the damage done was very trifling. The St. John's bell was rung, and a party galloped over to the School [Hampton Agricultural and Normal Institute] and [Soldiers] Home for assistance, but it was not necessary to bring either engine out. Fortunately it was very calm at the time of the fire, had it occurred an hour, or so later, nothing could have saved the entire structure from being burned down.

> In addition to the loss of the building, 13 beautiful white Pekin [*sic*] ducks, 65 grown chickens, and 16 young chicks were burned.
>
> The origin of the fire is not known, as there was no fire kept in either of the out-houses, and the servants say no ashes had been emptied there.
>
> One old colored man said after the fire, "I neber seed a white lady work so hard afore in my life; neber."

The next paragraph, without any warning of a change in topic, says "we are happy to announce" that the salary of the rector of St. John's Church "has been raised over fifty per cent; a deserved compliment to a faithful and earnest worker."

Wood scooped up all sorts of personal tidbits for the Union veterans to read: names of relatives visiting from out of town, church socials and Masonic events, and minutes of town council meetings. In September 1887 "the clerk was ordered to give 50 cents to the police to purchase meat for the dogs impounded."

The traditional source of news, the police blotter, furnished this item: "Mr. R. Massenburg, while under the influence of liquor, made an attack upon Mr. E. A. Semple on Saturday, in the drug store of H. R. Booker. He was arrested by officers Robinson and Randall before very much damage had been done, and carried before the Mayor, who fined him $10."

Massenburg's name was in the news again when readers were advised that he "was unfortunate enough to lose a valuable horse on Thursday. It had been sick but a short time. Part of the stable had to be knocked down in order to get the body out."

Most obituaries published in the *Home Bulletin* were straightforward, with a complimentary comment about deceased. This one, which has the imprint of George Wood's style, is different: "Mrs. Thumm, wife of the cap maker, living halfway between Hampton and the Point, died on Tuesday about 11 o'clock. The deceased was gored by a bull about a year ago, and has never been right well since. Mr. Thumm is the only Union solider we know of around here who stood guard in Hampton before it was burnt down."

In February 1886, Wood couldn't resist a small, albeit humorous, sermon: "A reader of the *Bulletin* says that during the recent cold snap a glass of toddy left in his room over night was frozen next morning. While admiring this striking evidence of self-denial in our friend, we hope it will be a warning to him; supposing the toddy had frozen in him instead of the tumbler, the community would have lost an esteemed citizen and the *Bulletin* a valued patron."

And there is this near tragedy that inspired a thoroughly original news account:

> The Virginia pilot boat was towed to the Soldiers Home wharf on Saturday afternoon to get out of the ice in the roads. While laying here, one of the young pilots attempted to cross the creek between the Home and School grounds, but,
>
> The ice it was thin,
> And Josey slipped in,
> And went up to his chin;
> He made a terrible din,
> But by pluck and vim,
> As he knew how to swim,
> Right side up he came out
> And turned him about,
> With a resolution that another time he would pilot his huge craft into a less dangerous harbor.

Wood served as secretary—as well as newspaper reporter—for a series of community meetings that in 1886 called for the incorporation of Hampton. He described the city's boundary as follows—"Beginning at the sycamore tree on Queen Street, north to Union Street, thence east to Little Back or Pee Dee Creek, around Hampton Creek to a line to and up Holt Street, west to opposite Sycamore and to sycamore tree." (The straight-line western boundary between the sycamore tree and Pee Dee Creek put St. John's Church outside the city.)

Hampton was incorporated in July 1887, and the council elected Captain John W. Brown as mayor. Wood approved. "We think," he wrote in the *Bulletin,* "the choice a very good one." Wood based his endorsement on the belief that Brown "will ever be on the alert for what will be the interest of the town and will see that things are conducted in an economical manner," and that he "will do his duty irrespective of party loyalty or personal feelings."

Then Wood inserted a bit of whimsy: "[B]eing an undertaker, should the town die of inanition [he] will see that funeral expenses are as economical as possible."

Wood freely offered his advice to council:

> We suggest to the new council that they, as soon as practicable, enact an ordinance eradicating the dog nuisance, which so sorely afflicts Hampton at the present time. A special tax on dogs and a general slaughter of all worthless canines would be a good remedy.
>
> Now that Hampton has become a city, it would be in order to specify a "road level" and compel property owners to conform to it. Then toe-stumbling and left-handed prayers would go out of fashion.

In 1883, after a romantic courtship fraught with an anxious period of mutual misunderstanding, George Wood married Annie Lee Bryon. The wedding took place in the bride's parents' home on April 25, 1883, the day of her twentieth birthday. The groom was thirty-five and a half. Annie Lee grew up in a rural area of Elizabeth City County known as Sawyer's Swamp, south of Big Bethel and so named because woodcutters worked there.

Mattie, apparently, was left to live alone—perhaps one reason why she disapproved of the marriage. Still, there were family members nearby. Residing in the immediate vicinity were Mattie's siblings, their spouses, and children: brothers Sam, Ned, and John, and a sister, Sallie Cake.

George Wood knew Annie Lee when she was a child because his brother Sam had married her older sister, Laura Jane Bryon. Laura died in 1873, and Sam married another Bryon sister, Margaret "Ellie" Bryan.

George and Annie Lee Wood had five children—Robert, born in 1884; Annie, who was called "Nannie," born in 1885; Georgie, called "Jean," born in 1888; Elvia, born in 1892; and Margaret, born in 1895.

From 1887 until her death in 1907, Annie Lee's mother, twice a widow, lived with her daughter and son-in-law. After Charles Bryon's death, Margaret Bryon married John Baines and continued to live in Sawyer's Swamp until he died.

The family lived in a house George and Annie Lee built at 301 Washington Street, one of the first homes in Pasture Point, a neighborhood immediately upstream from Pee Dee. Though altered, it stands today, at the intersection of Syms Street.

Years later, the Wood's daughter, Elvia Wood Curtis, wrote an untitled description of her life in the Wood family. Her parents, she recalled, were "great readers," and the family's social life centered on the church—Sunday school picnics, socials, and children's days. Her parents were fond of attending theatrical productions and amateur shows and participating in masquerades.

"All domestic work with the exception of needle work was done in the mornings," Elvia wrote, "and the afternoons were spent waiting for callers, reading or leisure. We had two elderly maiden cousins that would dress up in their best and go shopping every afternoon and on their way home would stop by our house and mother would serve them a cup of tea." These cousins, alas, remain unnamed.

Annie Lee Wood liked to entertain. "It gave her the greatest pleasure," Elvia remembered, "to put leaves in the table and set it with her pretty china and silver and feeding lots of people." Elvia claimed "the pantry was always filled" with cans of peas, corn, tomatoes, and asparagus. "Large pitchers of milk" and "fresh country eggs" were delivered to the door. There was even a wooden tub of chocolate drops.

Annie Lee and George had a cook, Amanda, who lived with them for seventeen years until she left to be married. "My mother furnished her whole house. She [Amanda] invited the family out to spend the day on her farm, and we went. She set the table with a snow-white cloth and everything was very neat. She wouldn't sit down with us, but stood and waited on us."

George Wood was active in political affairs as a Republican, a party affiliation that set him in the minority among whites in Hampton. His politics, which he did not discuss in his journal, apparently did not alienate him from friends and associates in the business community. So loyal was George Wood's dedication to the Republican Party that he remained at the polls on November 7, 1892, the day when Elvia was born.

In 1896 he organized and was president of the White Republican Club, an organization, he admitted, that "was not recognized for [its] splendid service," and after two years "was abolished."

Wood's partisanship was mocked by local Democrats who, buoyed by the election of President Woodrow Wilson in 1912, paraded through the streets with a hearse that represented Wood's political demise. As they marched past Wood's house,

George Randolph Wood later in life.
(Mariners' Museum)

Elvia remembered that "we turned out all the lights so we could have a better view of the solemn procession," which was led by Otto Lackey "dressed in his famous Uncle Sam costume."

George Wood had two fraternal commitments—one to the Odd Fellows Lodge where he was a member for fifty-two years and the other to St. Tammany Lodge No. 5, AF&AM. He was a Mason for fifty years and lodge president from June 1890 to June 1891. Wood was fond of telling this anecdote: "My wife wears a Masonic charm, and when asked if her husband is a Mason, she says, 'He is, and that most of those who are in his Lodge run against a 6-foot-2 wooden obstruction.'"

Early in 1917, for some unstated reason, Wood moved his drug store to 50 West Queen Street where, he advertised in the *Daily Press,* "I have for sale lawn grass, flower and garden seed and a good stock of drugs." He also dispensed "liquors for family use."

George Randolph Wood died "of paralysis" in his home at 4 p.m. on December 7, 1920. He was seventy-three.

After a service for the family conducted by the rector of St. John's Church, the Reverend E. R. Carter, the interment in the Episcopal church cemetery was carried out in accordance with the Masonic ritual. Eight of his nephews served as pallbearers and seventy-four friends and relatives were listed as honorary pallbearers. The *Daily Press* remarked that George Wood was "a descendant of two of the oldest families of Virginia."

Annie Lee Wood remained in her home on Washington Street as her health declined. She died of an apparent heart attack on June 18, 1928, at the age of sixty-five.

Appendix

Noteworthy Persons, Places, and Ships

Genealogy of the Wood Family of Hampton

There is no complete genealogy of Wood family members who lived in Hampton and Elizabeth City County during the nineteenth and early twentieth centuries, so biographical data for George Randolph Wood's ancestors, members of the extended Wood family, George's siblings, and even his children are incomplete. The information here has been assembled from family records placed in the library of The Mariners' Museum; from his granddaughter, Jacqueline Gaylord Milliken of Hampton; and from directories of cemeteries in Hampton and Virginia newspapers, principally the *Daily Press* of Newport News. Unfortunately, there is a gap in extant copies of the *Daily Press* between December 15, 1899, and January 6, 1905, and scattered other issues are missing as well.

George Randolph Wood's parents were Robert Clement Wood (August 4, 1804–June 7, 1864) and Susan Davis Hicks Wood (December 28, 1808–December 26, 1872). Both were born in Hampton, where they were married in 1826, and both are buried in St. John's Church Cemetery, Hampton. George was the tenth of their twelve children, who were as follows:

Mary Jane. Her birth date is unknown. She died in 1852 and at the time of her death was married to Robert Pope, who was born in 1827 in Nansemond County. Some time after Mary Jane's death he married her younger sister, Keturah Wood.

Martha Ann, also known as Mat and Mattie. Born June 1, 1829. She was unmarried and lived with her parents throughout the Civil War and in Hampton until they died. She helped raise her orphaned nephew, Jefferson Ward Wingfield. She died November 20, 1898, and is buried with her parents in St. John's Church Cemetery, Hampton.

Robert B. Born March 7, 1831. Before the Civil War he married Sarah Phillips (1836–1903) and lived in the Fox Hill section of Elizabeth City County. He was a Union sympathizer and in 1861 received a Federal appointment as "surveyor of the port of Hampton," but never took up the position. In August 1861 he was charged as a spy for the Union and imprisoned in Richmond. He was released in March 1863 and returned to Hampton. After the war Robert was "collector of internal revenue" for twenty years, and then Hampton's postmaster for three years. He died October 31, 1898, and is buried in Oakland Cemetery, Hampton.

John B., also called Jack. Born circa 1834. He enlisted in the Thirty-second Virginia Infantry Regiment and was stationed in Yorktown. He deserted in May 1862 and returned to Hampton to be with his wife, Christiana. Census records for 1860, 1870, and 1880 list him as a house carpenter. He died in 1893.

William A., known as Billy. Born September 15, 1835. At the outbreak of the Civil War he was married to Melissa Massenburg. In July 1861, he joined the Thirty-second Virginia Infantry Regiment and was stationed at Yorktown where he was injured while handling a mortar. He went to City Point to be with his wife, who had evacuated Hampton. The couple returned to Hampton by November 1862. While the date of his death can not be determined, it is known that he was living in 1911.

Keturah, also spelled Kathurah and Ketura. Born circa 1839. At the outbreak of the Civil War she was married to Robert Pope, who enlisted in July 1861 in the Thirty-second Virginia Infantry Regiment. Keturah Pope accompanied her parents to City Point and returned to Hampton with them in 1864. Robert Pope deserted and took the oath of allegiance to the United States on July 13, 1864, returning to his home on the Back River in Elizabeth City County. The 1880 census lists him as a house painter, and the family was then living in Norfolk. It is unknown when either Keturah or Robert Pope died.

Elizabeth. Her birth date is unknown. At the time of the Civil War she was married to Joseph Wingfield of Hanover County. Elizabeth

Wingfield accompanied her parents to City Point with her infant son, Jefferson Ward Wingfield, born in Hampton on March 19, 1861. She died later that year and is buried at City Point. George Wood makes no references to her husband in his account.

Sarah Frances, known as "Sallie" and "Sally". Born January 9, 1842. She accompanied her parents to City Point and later, while living in Richmond, married Charles Davis Cake of Hampton, who had enlisted in the Hampton Grays and served in Thirty-second Virginia Infantry Regiment. Their son, George R. Cake, was born at Weston on April 30, 1864. Though Cake's military record is spotty, he was recorded as twice absent without leave in 1862 and again in 1863. He deserted in June 1864 and took an oath of amnesty. After the war, Cake supervised the sawmill and the woodworking department at Hampton Normal and Agricultural Institute and in 1886 moved to Norfolk. Sallie Cake died April 8, 1907, and she and her husband are buried in St. John's Church Cemetery, Hampton.

Samuel B. Born September 9, 1845. He accompanied his parents throughout the Civil War and served with the Confederate Transportation Department on river barges, at times with his father and his brother George. After he returned to Hampton he married Laura Jane Bryon, and on her death in 1873, he married her younger sister, Margaret Elvy "Ellie" Bryon. The 1880 census lists him as a grocer. In 1887, he placed advertisements in the *Soldiers Home Bulletin* as a representative of the Life Insurance Company of Virginia, offering "poor man gets insurance 10 to 75 cents a week." He served as a magistrate, clerk of the circuit court, and a member of the school board. He died January 1, 1911, and is buried in St. John's Church Cemetery, Hampton.

George Randolph. Born on November 7, 1847. When he returned to Hampton in 1864 and was released from prison camp, he lived with his mother until she died in 1872. On April 25, 1883, George married Annie Lee Bryon (April 25, 1863–June 18, 1928), the youngest sister of his sister-in-law, Ellie Bryon Wood. They had four children. After working as a blacksmith, George was a clerk in several stores and for a time in 1875 worked for Harrison Phoebus at the Hygeia Hotel on

Old Point Comfort. In 1878 George partnered with Henry Clay Whiting, a successful older businessman, and together they opened a grocery and drug store; seven years later George was a licensed pharmacist. George died December 7, 1920, and is buried with his wife in St. John's Church Cemetery, Hampton.

Edward Hicks, also known as Ned and Ed. Born in 1849. He remained with his parents throughout the Civil War. Sometime shortly after his mother died in 1872, he married Imogene Smith (1852–1886). The 1880 census lists him as a ship carpenter. He died in 1914 and is buried with his wife in St. John's Church Cemetery, Hampton.

Emma Virginia. Born June 29, 1850. She remained with her parents throughout the Civil War. She married John Wesley Richardson, the widower of a cousin, Annie Wood, and a Confederate veteran. He was mayor of Hampton from 1894 to 1900, and after he died in 1911 she moved to Greenville, Kentucky, where she died on April 27, 1934. Both she and her husband are buried in St. John's Church Cemetery, Hampton.

The children of George Randolph and Annie Lee Bryon Wood were as follows:

Robert "Rob" E. Wood. Born January 31, 1884, date of death unknown. A pharmacist, he married Nannie L. Copeland on March 26, 1913.

Annie "Nannie" M. Wood. Born June 20, 1885, died April 23, 1939. She married Harry Shields Cunningham (1883–1945), an undertaker, on August 31, 1905. She is buried in St. John's Church Cemetery, Hampton.

Georgie "Jean" Rowena Wood. Born December 17, 1888, died April 23, 1963. She married Robert Lee Gaylord (1873–1929), a justice of the peace, on November 11, 1911. After his death she married Edward Allen Stern, whose birth and death dates are unknown. She is buried in the Hampton National Cemetery.

Elvia Theresa Wood. Born November 7, 1892, died July 8, 1977. She married Thomas Sinclair Curtis (1886–1937), deputy sheriff of Elizabeth City County, on June 24, 1925. She is buried in St. John's Church Cemetery, Hampton

Margaret Adelaid Wood. Born September 8, 1895, died February 10, 1973. She married Samuel Bee Woodward, a physician in Dayton, Ohio, and after his death married Leon B. Stayton of Wilmington, Delaware.

Persons of Note

Captain George W. Alexander, a native of Pennsylvania, resigned from the U.S. Navy to join the Confederate army and commanded the prison Castle Godwin in Richmond. He was author of *The Virginia Cavalier* and other wartime plays staged in Richmond. Although *The Virginia Cavalier* was the greatest hit of the Confederate stage, the *Southern Illustrated News* called it "the sorriest sight of all."

Dr. Joseph K. Barnes, who cared for Sallie Cake and her baby in May 1864, was appointed the Union army's surgeon general that summer. He attended the mortally wounded Abraham Lincoln, performed the autopsy on the president's assassin, Edwin Booth, and, in 1881, treated President James A. Garfield after he was shot by an assassin.

Robert B. Blassingham, a Williamsburg merchant who operated a business at Grove Wharf, purchased the Raleigh Tavern in 1857, which burned two years later under suspicious circumstances. Some people thought Blassingham may have set the fire to collect insurance money. In 1860 Blassingham was accused of forgery; the resolution of this is unknown.

Richard M. Booker, the Confederate officer who allegedly accused Robert B. Wood of drawing a map for Federal soldiers, was captured in Amelia County, Virginia, in the spring of 1864. After the war he was a deputy sheriff of Elizabeth City County, an auctioneer, a brickmaker, and a road builder. He died February 11, 1898, and is buried in St. John's Church Cemetery, Hampton.

Robert Anderson Bright, a resident of Williamsburg, was an officer with the Fifty-third Virginia Infantry Regiment until he was detailed to the staff of General George Pickett. Bright surrendered at Appomattox and after the Civil War was an outspoken opponent of equal rights for black citizens.

George Robert Cake, son of Sarah "Sallie" Wood and Charles D. Cake, was born at Weston, Prince George County, on April 30, 1864, and died of consumption in Hampton on October 19, 1885.

Hill Carter of Shirley Plantation in Charles City County, served in the U.S. Navy during the War of 1812. At the start of the Civil War he, at the age of sixty-five, held a colonelcy in the Virginia Militia and commanded infantry in defense of Jamestown Island until it was abandoned on May 3, 1862. Thereafter he remained neutral in order to protect the family's estate.

John Baytop Cary, a descendant of Miles Cary (who settled in Warwick County in 1640), was graduated from William and Mary in 1839 and in 1852 established the Hampton Male and Female Academy, a college preparatory school that offered a military curriculum. It is claimed that more than thirty Confederate officers received their initial military training at Cary's Military Academy. During the Civil War, Cary was assistant paymaster for the Confederate army. Afterward, he lived in Richmond and owned an insurance agency. He died there January 12, 1898, and is buried in Hollywood Cemetery.

Marion Colbert ran a book and stationery shop on Queen Street near King in Hampton after the Civil War. He was a state officer in the International Order of Odd Fellows. He died in 1907 and is buried in St. John's Church Cemetery, Hampton.

Charles Henry Collier of Hampton, "author" of the rebel yell, enlisted May 13, 1861, at age nineteen and served in Company A, Thirty-second Virginia Regiment, until May 2, 1862, when he was transferred to the navy. After the Civil War he was superintendent of public education in Memphis, Tennessee.

John Alexander Curtis, the boatman from Hampton who served as superintendent of transportation on the James River and Kanawha Canal, was involved in spying on the James River. He participated in a torpedo boat attack on the USS *Minnesota* and an expedition to free prisoners from Point Lookout, Maryland. Subsequently, he served briefly aboard the CSS *Tallahassee.* Late in the war he was detailed to spy on Fort Monroe. After the Civil War he was a ship broker in Richmond.

Richard A. Curtis initially enlisted in the Thirty-second Virginia Regiment and was transferred on January 30, 1862, to the Confederate navy to serve aboard the CSS *Virginia*. In 1907, when he was living in Norfolk, he wrote the pamphlet *History of the Famous Battle Between the Iron-Clad* Merrimac, *C.S.N., and the Iron-Clad* Monitor *and the* Cumberland *and* Congress *of the U.S. Navy*. He died April 22, 1926, the last surviving crew member of the CSS *Virginia*.

William T. Daougherty of Hampton, who after the Civil War married Mary Curtis, rode as a cavalryman with Jeb (James Ewell Brown) Stuart and participated in more than thirty-five engagements and battles. He was captured at Front Royal in August 1864 and was paroled in March 1865. After the war he was a builder, responsible for, among other projects, the famous Hygeia Hotel at Old Point Comfort. In 1895 he was elected commissioner of revenue for Hampton, a post he held until his death in 1905.

General John Gray Foster commanded the U.S. Army's Department of Virginia and North Carolina from July 11, 1863, to November 11, 1863, and was headquartered at Fort Monroe.

E. G. Ghio was superintendent of the Seaboard and Roanoke Railroad after the Civil War.

William A. Graves, a Norfolk shipbuilder, was a naval constructor for the Confederate navy at Richmond. After the Civil War he resumed his shipbuilding business in Norfolk and served on the city council. He was a director of the Virginia Pilots Association when he died in 1894.

Brigadier General Edward Ward Hincks commanded the African American troops that landed at City Point on May 5, 1864. He was the governor (superintendent) of the National Home for Disabled Volunteers in Hampton between 1870 and 1873.

Major Kensey Johns was the son of John Johns, the Episcopal bishop of Virginia from 1842 until his death in 1876, and president of the College of William and Mary from 1849 until 1854. Kensey, who lived with his father in Ashland during the Civil War, was in charge of river and canal transportation and operated from an office at the river dock in Richmond.

Catesby ap Roger Jones, a Confederate naval officer who was employed in the conversion of the steam frigate USS *Merrimack* into the Confederate ironclad *Virginia,* was the ship's executive officer and in command on March 9, 1862, during the historic engagement with the USS *Monitor.*

Charles K. Mallory, a prominent Hampton lawyer, was elected to represent Elizabeth City County and adjoining Peninsula jurisdictions in the Secession Convention of April 1861. He held a state commission as a colonel in command of the 115th Militia Regiment and served as a captain in the Confederate army's Quartermaster Corps. He was the owner of the three runaway slaves that Major General Benjamin F. Butler protected at Fort Monroe as the first contraband of war.

Richard DeOrsey Ogden, stage manger and performer at the Richmond Theater, was a British citizen and unsympathetic to the cause of the Confederacy. As a result, he was unpopular in the Southern press and with Confederate soldiers. During one performance, when his character said "I will go back to England," a soldier in the audience yelled out, "You had better go or you will lose your British protection."

Sallie Partington, a leading singer and stage actress in Richmond during and after the Civil War, was born in England, died in Richmond on January 10, 1907, at the age of seventy-three, and is buried in Hollywood Cemetery. In reporting her death, the *Richmond Times-Dispatch* said "she was an ornament to the profession and a high-minded woman." She and her sister, Mary, also a stage actress, were favorites of Confederate President Jefferson Davis.

Flag Officer J. Garrett Pendergrast commanded the sloop USS *Cumberland* and a small flotilla that, at the outbreak of the Civil War in 1861, seized Confederate ships and privateers in Hampton Roads. Pendergrast was married to Virginia Barron, daughter of Commodore James Barron, a native of Hampton. She was a staunch supporter of the Confederacy.

Francis Anton Schmelz, who emigrated from Germany, ran a bakery and confectionery on Queen Street in Hampton and became a wealthy man. He died on December 7, 1881, and is buried in St. John's Church Cemetery. His sons, George A. and Henry L. Schmelz, established a privately owned bank that financed much of the postwar economic growth in Hampton and, later, in Newport News.

Arthur Simpkins Segar, who was three years older than George Wood, fought in the Civil War and was wounded at Gettysburg and Drewry's Bluff. He opened a law practice in 1874 and was commonwealth's attorney for Elizabeth City County before he died in 1901.

George William Semple, surgeon for the Thirty-second Virginia Infantry Regiment, who was later in charge of prison hospitals in Richmond, was born in York County in 1812. He was a graduate of William and Mary and the University of Pennsylvania, and practiced medicine in Alabama and Charles City County before establishing a practice in Hampton in 1846. He was president of the Medical Society of Virginia in 1881. He died in November 15, 1883, and is buried in St. John's Church Cemetery, Hampton. The inscription on his tombstone reads: "The Beloved Physician."

Henry Clay Whiting, a prominent Hampton businessman, bank president, and city councilman, was George Wood's business partner in a grocery and drug store starting in 1878. He was born December 24, 1832, in Elizabeth City County, the son of Kennon Whiting. During the Civil War, Whiting initially served as an officer in the Thirty-second Virginia Infantry Regiment and later as a staff officer with the Army of Tennessee, and surrendered April 26, 1865, in North Carolina. He may once have been on the staff of General William Henry Chase Whiting of North Carolina (though if there was family relationship, it can not be determined). He died January 18, 1899, and is buried in St. John's Church Cemetery, Hampton.

Jefferson Ward Wingfield, George's nephew (also known as Jeff and Jessie, and later in life to the general public as "Captain Jeff"), was a popular motorman for the Newport News and Hampton Railway, Gas and Electric Company. He was born in Hampton on March 19, 1861, and before the year was ended his mother, Elizabeth Wood Wingfield, died at City Point. Raised by his unmarried aunt, Martha Wood, he lived in Hampton where he died on January 9, 1921, at age fifty-nine. He is buried in St. John's Church Cemetery, Hampton.

Brevet Major General John E. Wool succeeded Major General Benjamin F. Butler as commander of the military Department of Virginia with headquarters at Fort Monroe. He served from August 17, 1861, to June 2, 1862. Fort Calhoun on the Rip Rap Shoal in Hampton Roads was renamed Fort Wool in his honor.

Places of Note

Note: For the locations of many of the places that follow, refer to the six maps that appear in the text on pp. 8, 50, 64, 74, 86, and 108.

Aiken's (also Atken's or Atkin's) Landing, Henrico County. *See* Varina, Henrico County.

Appomattox River. For 10 miles between Petersburg and its confluence with the James River at City Point, the river is navigable, but restricted to a depth of 5½ feet between Petersburg and Port Walthall.

Back River, Hampton. Two principal branches—one from the southwest (New Market Creek) and the other from the northwest—join to form the Back River to the north of nineteenth-century Hampton. The short tidal river empties into the Chesapeake Bay.

Back River, Jamestown Island. The waterway that separates Jamestown Island and the mainland of James City County was, in colonial times, often referred to as the Thoroughfare.

Back River Road, Hampton. This road extended northward from West Hampton to a bridge across New Market Creek located downstream from the older New Market bridge.

Beechwood, Prince George County. One of Edmund Ruffin's farms, Beechwood was located at Coggin's Point on the James River. Here Ruffin carried out his initial agricultural experiments using marl, a crumbly mixture of clay, sand, limestone, and remnants of shells used as fertilizer for lime-deficient soils.

Bermuda Hundred. This tract of low land between the James and Appomattox rivers was named by Sir Thomas Gates to commemorate the time he spent shipwrecked in Bermuda while en route to Virginia in 1609. Today it is the site of industrial plants.

Blackbeard's Point, Hampton. The severed head of Edward Teach, the infamous pirate known as Blackbeard, was spiked on pole erected in 1718 at the entranceway to the port of Hampton as a warning to pirates. The spot in present-day Hampton is at the end of Ivy Home Road.

Blandford. A small eighteenth-century community, Blandford was incorporated as part of Petersburg in 1784. Blandford Church was the object of the Union attack July 30, 1864, in the Battle of the Crater, but was never reached. Approximately 30,000 Confederate soldiers are buried in the Blandford Church cemetery, believed to be the site of the first Confederate Memorial Day observance, held in June 1866.

Broadway, Prince George County. This community on the Appomattox River was laid out in 1700 by Thomas Broadway and was an important landing early in the nineteenth century. Federal troops erected a pontoon bridge across the Appomattox there in 1864.

Bonsack. A community to the northeast of Roanoke.

Camp Page, Williamsburg. A Confederate encampment, Camp Page was located along the road between the city and College Landing on College Creek.

Cawsons (also Cawson's), Prince George County. The ancestral home of the Bland family on the Appomattox River, Cawsons is the birthplace of John Randolph, who served in the U.S. Senate from 1825 to 1827.

Chaffin Bluff (also Chaffin's) . This sixty-foot high bluff sits on the north side of the James River downstream from Drewry's Bluff. Confederates were driven off on September 29, 1864, and Union soldiers fortified Chaffin Bluff and attempted to neutralize the Confederates across the river at Drewry's Bluff.

Chesapeake Female College. Established in 1857 in a five-story building overlooking Hampton Roads, the Chesapeake Female College was one the principal seminaries in Virginia before the Civil War. The main building was used by the Union army as a hospital. The property was acquired in 1864 by General Benjamin Butler, who sold it to the federal government for a Soldiers Home for Union veterans. Today it is the site of the Veterans Administration Hospital.

Chickahominy River. A tributary of the James River with swampy headwaters northeast of Richmond, the Chickahominy was navigable in the nineteenth century for about thirty miles to Rockahock.

City Point. Settled in 1613, this community at the confluence of the

Appomattox and James rivers was originally part of Charles City County when it was named Charles City Point. Early in the eighteenth century the point became part of Prince George County and the name was abbreviated to City Point. When a railroad connected City Point with Petersburg in 1836, the hamlet was a major transfer point for passengers and freight. On May 5, 1864, the Union army occupied City Point and on June 15 General Grant established his headquarters there at Appomattox Manor. The army built wharves, warehouses, and hospitals and established a supply depot for the 115,000-man Army of the Potomac that lay siege to Petersburg.

Claremont, Surry County. A community on the southern bank of the James River, Claremont was an important river landing in the era of steamboats. Major Arthur Allen of Bacon's Castle originally patented the land in the 1670s. His son, John Allen, built a home there early in the eighteenth century. Colonel William Allen owned Claremont when he died in 1832 and was the wealthiest man in Virginia. He left his fortune to his nephew, Richard Orgain, on condition that the boy change his name to William Allen. Orgain, renamed Allen, owned vast acreages along the James River, including Jamestown Island where he had a house in the 1850s. Claremont flourished after the Civil War, but was in decline when George Wood visited there in 1906.

Coggin's Point, Prince George County. Also known as Ruffin's Bluff, this is the site of Edmund Ruffin's Beechwood farm. It was from here in early July 1862 that Ruffin watched General George B. McClellan's Army of the Potomac encamp at Berkeley Plantation across the James River, and from this bluff Confederate General Daniel Harvey Hill bombarded the Federals on July 31.

Curles Neck. Between Varina and the mouth of the Appomattox River, the James River curls in a series of tight bends, some nearly full circle. On the north bank, the peninsula once owned by Nathaniel Bacon is known was Curles Neck.

Drewry's Bluff. Confederate fortifications on the southern side of the James River, in a bluff owned by Captain A. H. Drewry, blocked Union gunboats from attacking Richmond, about six miles upstream.

Electric Road, Hampton. A principal twentieth-century road between Hampton and Newport News used by electric trolley cars. Today it is known as Victoria Boulevard.

Eppes Island, Charles City County. Considered by the Virginia Division of Historic Landmarks as possibly the oldest farm in Virginia, Eppes Island was first cultivated by the Eppes family in 1624. It is located in the vicinity of Shirley Plantation on the northern bank of the James River opposite Bermuda Hundred.

Fox Hill, Hampton. This rural community in Elizabeth City County straddles present-day Beach Road on a peninsula bounded by Harris Creek, the Back River, and the Chesapeake Bay.

Gallego Mills, Richmond. Established in 1796 by Joseph Gallego, this water-powered flour mill was located at the turn basin of the James River and Kanawha Canal. Before the Civil War, it was one of the largest mills in the United States, with a major trade with South America and California. It was burned during the evacuation fire of 1865, and subsequently rebuilt.

Grove Wharf, James City County. Prior to the Civil War, this busy wharf at Carter's Grove plantation was a principal steamboat landing serving Williamsburg.

Harrison's Bar. This sandbar in the James River below City Point and opposite Harrison's Landing restricted shipping to a depth of sixteen feet.

Harrison's Landing, Charles City County. On the northern bank of the James River, Harrison's Landing served Berkeley Plantation, where the Army of the Potomac encamped following the Seven Days Campaign in 1862.

Haxall Mills, Richmond. Established by Philip Haxall, this was a major flour mill located at the turn basin of the James River and Kanawha Canal. It was rebuilt after the evacuation fire of 1865.

Haxall's Landing, Charles City County. This landing at Haxall Farm is on the northern bank of the James River above Shirley and opposite the Turkey Island peninsula.

Howlett's Farm, Chesterfield County. Situated on a bluff on the southern side of the James River above Dutch Gap, here a Confederate artillery battery anchored a defensive line built in 1864 to contain

General Benjamin Butler's Army of the James when it occupied Bermuda Hundred. The four-mile-long line extended southward to Port Walthall Junction and was known as the Howlett Line.

Jamestown Island. This site of the first permanent English settlement in America was the capital of Virginia for ninety-two years and then largely abandoned. During the Civil War the island was owned by William Allen and, after May 5, 1862, occupied for the remainder of the war as a Union outpost. A bridge crossed the Back River, also known as the Thoroughfare, leading to Williamsburg.

John's Creek, Hampton. A small tidal creek, now largely filled in, John's Creek lies near the mouth of the Hampton River on the north side draining from an area to the west of Camp Hamilton, later developed as Chesapeake City and renamed Phoebus. The mouth of John's Creek is between Jones Creek and Mill Creek.

Jones Creek, Hampton. This small tidal creek, now largely filed in, lies on the north side of the Hampton River upstream from John's Creek and marked the western boundary of the Chesapeake Female Academy, which after the Civil War became the site of the Soldiers Home for Union veterans. A wharf on Jones Creek, sometimes known as College Creek, served Hampton Institute when that school was established after the Civil War. The prison encampment where George Wood was detained in 1864 was located along the east side of Jones Creek.

Jones Landing. Although not identified on extant James River maps of the Civil War period, George Wood locates this landing "opposite Varina" on Jones Neck.

Maidens Adventure, Goochland County. Nowadays simply called Maidens, the settlement on the north bank of the James River takes its name from the legend of a girl who, in colonial times, crossed the James River to warn her sweetheart of an imminent Indian attack.

Metropolitan Theater. One of several wartime theaters in Richmond, the Metropolitan was located on East Franklin Street.

Mill Point, Hampton. After the Civil War, George Wood's brother-in-law, Charles Cake, established a mill on the site of Cary's Military Academy, which was destroyed in the fire of 1861. Since then, that spot along the Hampton River, once part of the Pee Dee neighborhood, has been known as Mill Point. Today it is a residential area.

Mulberry Island, Warwick County. This peninsula, formed by the Warwick and James rivers, was named by Captain John Smith in 1610 for the wild mulberry trees growing there. One of the first places settled after Jamestown, today it is part of Newport News and the site of Fort Eustis.

New Market Road, Hampton. A westward extension of West Queen Street, New Market Road leads to a bridge over New Market Creek, a tributary of the Southwest Branch of the Back River.

Pagan River. The town of Smithfield in Isle of Wight County sits on the Pagan River 4½ miles from where this tidal waterway meets the James River.

Pocahontas. Situated on the northern side of the Appomattox River opposite Petersburg, this community was the southern terminus of the Richmond and Petersburg Railroad. A railroad bridge across the river just upstream from the city wharf was built in 1863.

Richmond Theater. Originally called the Marshall Theater, the playhouse at 701 East Broad Street was renovated in 1860 and renamed the Richmond Theater. It was destroyed on January 2, 1862, by a mysterious fire that the theater's manager, John Hill Hewitt, believed to be arson. The second Richmond Theater, a handsome five-story building with promenade, dress circle, and cast-iron scrollwork, was built on the same site and opened on February 9, 1863, with a performance of Shakespeare's *As You Like It.* The last wartime performance there was given on April 2, 1865, but the theater reopened two days later for patronage by Union officers.

Rockahock (also Rockahoc or Rock-a-hock), New Kent County. A landing on the Chickahominy River at the end of Old New Kent Road from Slatersville. On Johnson's map of 1862 Rockahock is called Sherman's Place and labeled Steamboat Landing.

Rocketts. The farthest navigable point on the James River, Rocketts is below the rocky falls at Richmond where Robert and Charles Rocketts operated a ferry in the eighteenth century.

Roseland Manor. Built in 1887 by wealthy hotelier Harrison Phoebus,

Roseland Manor was a major landmark on the Hampton River before it was destroyed by fire in 1985.

Rowland's Mill, Charles City County. The Wood family briefly lived in a house here in the spring of 1862. That summer the Rowland house served as headquarters for Union generals Erasmus Darwin Keyes and Edwin Vose Sumner. Today the house is known as Edgewood.

Ruffin's Bluff. *See* Coggin's Point, Prince George County.

Sailors Tavern. The location of this riverside tavern mentioned by George Wood is unknown, though there was a tavern at the former village of Warwick on the south side of the James River below Richmond.

Ship's Point, York County. This Confederate lookout post on the Chesapeake Bay was situated at the confluence of Chisman Creek and the Poquoson River and opposite York Point.

Shirley Wharf, Charles City County. This wharf on the north side of the James River served Shirley Plantation, which was opposite the landing at Bermuda Hundred. Shirley was the home of Hill Carter.

Slab Town. This community of ramshackle dwellings occupied by blacks was located across Mill Creek from Fort Monroe. The term also was applied to squatter neighborhoods in Hampton after the 1861 fire.

Spratley's, James City County. A farm established in the eighteenth century by John Spratley and kept in his family until after the Civil War, Spratley's was located on the James River upstream from the mouth of College Creek and between Archer's Hope and the James City Glebe. Confederate artillery emplacements were built there to guard the James River.

Tar Bay (also Tarbay), Prince George County. This plantation adjacent to Beechwood on Coggin's Point was owned by Thomas Cocke, Edmund Ruffin's guardian and mentor, and later by the Ruffin family. The main house faces Tar Bay, a wide-mouthed bay on the southern shore of the James River.

Varina, Henrico County. This community on the north side of the James River is named for a type of Spanish tobacco grown there and is said to have been at one time the residence of John Rolfe and

Pocahontas. It was an important prisoner exchange point during the Civil War, when it was known as Aiken's Landing.

Warwick. This village was established in 1660 below Richmond on the south bank of the James River, just above Falling Creek where the channel approached the southern shore. Incorporated in 1748, it became Richmond's principal tobacco port and a supply point for the Virginia State Navy during the American Revolution. The British under Benedict Arnold destroyed the military stores there in 1781, when the village was abandoned and the houses gradually torn down.

Warwick Bar. Five miles below Richmond, the Warwick Bar restricted vessels on the James River to a draft of twelve feet.

Warwick Town or Courthouse. One of the original shires, Warwick was established by the Virginia General Assembly on the Warwick River just inside the tip of Mulberry Island in 1680.

Watkins Landing, Prince George County. Watkins Farm is located on the southern bank of the James River south of Turkey Island and opposite Curles Neck.

Weston. Built circa 1735 on the Appomattox River, the manor house is one of the oldest residences in continuous use in Virginia and is on the National Register of Historic Places. During the Civil War, a cannon ball fired from a Union warship went through the dining room ceiling. After the family of Robert C. Wood vacated it in 1864, Union General Philip Sheridan briefly made the house his headquarters. Today, Weston is owned by the Historic Hopewell Foundation and is open to the public from April through October.

Westover, Charles City County. The colonial estate of William Byrd II, Westover is located on the northern bank of the James River below Berkeley.

Weyanoke, Charles City County. Weyanoke, a 1,225-acre peninsula on the northern bank of the James River, was occupied by Union General Philip Sheridan's troops in 1864 during the Battle of Cold Harbor, and was the site of a pontoon bridge across which 15,000 Union soldiers marched toward Petersburg.

Wilcox (also Willcox), Charles City County. General U. S. Grant's Union army crossed the James River on a pontoon bridge at this landing on June 14–16, 1864, at the outset of the Petersburg Campaign.

Ships of Note

Note: Hundreds of small boats—unpowered barges, steam tugs and small transports, schooners and sloops of various configurations—plied the currents and tides of the James and Appomattox rivers, few of them noted by newspapers or official records. Therefore, there are no apparent descriptions or accounts of service performed by such barges as the *William Coggin* or the tug *Banner*—or even the transport *Lady Lincoln*—mentioned by George Wood.

USS *Aroostook.* A 691-ton screw steam gunboat built in Kennebunk, Maine, and commissioned in Boston in February 1862, the *Aroostook* was armed with two 24-pound smoothbores, one 11-inch Dahlgren, and one 20-pound Parrott rifle. After participating in the May 1862 Battle of Drewry's Bluff, the ship was assigned blockade duty in the Gulf of Mexico until the end of the war.

CSS *Beaufort.* A propeller-driven iron tug of 85 tons built in 1854 at Wilmington, Delaware, the *Beaufort* was acquired by North Carolina in July 1861, and turned over to the Confederate navy on September 9. The tug participated in battles at Roanoke Island in February 1862 and was a coal tender for CSS *Virginia* in the Battle of Hampton Roads on March 8–9, 1862. Capable of moving in depths of just under seven feet, the *Beaufort* operated on the James River throughout the war, then was captured by the U.S. Navy at Richmond and sold in September 1865 for use as a merchant vessel.

USS *Commodore Barney.* A side-wheel New York City ferryboat acquired by the Federal government in October 1861. From July 1862 to March 1864 the *Commodore Barney* operated in and out of Hampton Roads. The vessel was damaged on August 5, 1863, on the James River above Dutch Gap, by the concussion of a thousand-pound electronic torpedo set off prematurely by Confederates on the riverbank, and roughly twenty men were washed overboard, two of whom were lost. When the *Barney* retreated downstream, it was hit more than thirty times by Confederate artillery fire, and the boiler was disabled.

USS *Congress*. A frigate, the USS *Congress* was attacked, set on fire, and destroyed off Newport News Point by the CSS *Virginia* on March 8, 1862, the first day of the Battle of the Ironclads.

USS *Cumberland*. A large sloop of war, the USS *Cumberland* was attacked, rammed, and sunk by the CSS *Virginia* off Newport News Point on March 8, 1862, the first day of the Battle of the Ironclads.

CSS *Curtis Peck*. A fast side-wheel steamer built in 1842 at New York and employed by the Confederacy as a reconnaissance ship on the James River in 1861, the *Curtis Peck* operated as a flag-of-truce boat in May 1862, delivering exchanged Union prisoners to Fort Monroe. The ship was scuttled in September 1862 to obstruct the James River below Drewry's Bluff.

USS *Galena*. An ironclad built in Mystic, Connecticut, and commissioned April 21, 1862, in the New York Navy Yard, the *Galena* was armed with four 9-inch Dahlgren smooth-bores and two 100-pound Parrott rifles, displaced 738 tons, and had a maximum speed of eight knots. The ship was severely damaged during the May 15, 1862, Battle of Drewry's Bluff, and was sent to Philadelphia in 1863 for repairs and removal of its iron plating. The *Galena* subsequently served as wooden gunboat in the Gulf of Mexico and, for a brief time at the end of the war, was a patrol ship in the lower James River.

CSS *Gallego*. A 596-ton schooner built in 1855 at Newburyport, Massachusetts, the *Gallego* was primarily employed as a cargo and store ship on the James River. Badly in need of repairs, the schooner was run aground below the obstructions at Drewry's Bluff in late 1864, but then refloated and stationed at Drewry's Bluff.

Glen Cove. A Confederate side-wheel steamer of 504 tons built in New York City in 1854, the *Glen Cove* was destroyed by fire on the James River in May 1861.

James Buchanan. A Confederate schooner, the *Buchanan* was commanded by Robert C. Wood and used on the James River to transport supplies.

Jamestown. *See* CSS *Thomas Jefferson*.

J. E. Coffee, also known as *Joseph E. Coffee*. A side-wheel steamer of 207 tons that operated out of Norfolk before the Civil War, the *J. E. Coffee* was purchased by North Carolina, renamed the *Winslow,* and turned over to the Confederate States Navy. The ship cruised off Hatteras Inlet, North Carolina, seizing Federal merchant ships, but was lost on November 7, 1861, near Ocracoke Inlet, after striking a sunken hulk.

USS *Maratanza.* A 786-ton "double-ender" steam gunboat commissioned in Boston in April 1862, for the next five months the *Maratanza* operated in the James and York rivers, bombarding Confederate positions and capturing the Confederate gunboat *Teaser* on July 4.

USS *Merrimack. See* CSS *Virginia.*

USS *Monitor.* After participating in the Battle of the Ironclads (also known as the Battle of Hampton Roads) on March 8–9, 1862, the *Monitor,* which had a draft of ten feet, six inches, ascended the James River to participate in the May 15 Battle of Drewry's Bluff, then returned to Hampton Roads for repairs and alterations. The ironclad sank in a storm in the Atlantic off Cape Hatteras on December 31, 1862, while being towed to Wilmington, North Carolina.

CSS *Nansemond.* A small wooden twin-screw steamer of 166 tons built at Norfolk in 1862, the *Nansemond* was assigned to the James River Squadron and took part in engagements at Howlett's on June 21, 1864; Dutch Gap on August 14, 1864; and Fort Harrison, from September 29 to October 1, 1864. The vessel was scuttled during the evacuation of Richmond on April 3, 1865.

USS *Naugatuck,* also known as *Stevens Battery.* A twin-screw gunboat of 192 tons built by Edwin A. Stevens of Hoboken, New Jersey, to demonstrate new warship technology, the *Naugatuck* was presented to the U.S. Revenue Service, which loaned the ship to the navy. In 1862 the ship engaged Confederate river batteries along the James. Damaged while attacking Drewry's Bluff on May 15, 1862, where its rifled gun blew up, the *Naugatuck* was returned to the Revenue Service.

New York. A propeller-driven steamer chartered by the Federal government, the *New York* served as a transport for the exchange of prisoners of war on the James River.

CSS *Northampton.* A side-wheel steamer of 405 tons built in 1860 in Baltimore and purchased by Virginia in June 1861, the *Northampton* was used as a cargo ship on the James River before being scuttled in May 1862 to block the James River channel below Drewry's Bluff.

CSS *Patrick Henry* (formerly the steamer *Yorktown*). A side-wheel steamer of 1,300 tons built in 1859 for the New York and Old Dominion Steamship Line, the *Yorktown* was seized by the state of Virginia on April 17, 1861, refitted as a gunboat, and renamed the *Patrick Henry.* Thereafter, the steamer was used as a training ship for Confederate midshipmen and scuttled at Rocketts in April 1865 to prevent its capture.

USS *Pennsylvania.* A ship of the line built in 1821, the *Pennsylvania* was deliberately burned April 20, 1861, at Gosport Navy Yard in Norfolk.

Plume. A pilot schooner serving Hampton Roads, owned by Robert C. Wood, Charles Topping, Thomas Cunningham, James Hicks, and Edmund Rudd, the *Plume* was one of five such weatherly craft owned by pilots living in Hampton immediately before the Civil War. The others were the *Reindeer, Antelope, Hope,* and *York.*

USS *Port Royal.* A gunboat of 805 tons commissioned in April 1862 at the Brooklyn Navy Yard, the *Port Royal* was armed with one 100-pound Parrott, one 10-inch Dahlgren smoothbore, and six 24-pound howitzers.

CSS *Raleigh.* A steam tug, the *Raleigh* served as a dispatch boat running between Richmond and City Point.

CSS *Schultz,* also known as *A. H. Schultz.* A side-wheel steamer of 164 tons built in New York City, the *Schultz* served as a Confederate flag-of-truce boat on the James River. The ship was accidentally blown up by a Confederate torpedo that drifted loose from the barricades at Drewry's Bluff and sank on February 9, 1865.

Seaboard. A side-wheel wooden tug of 59 tons built at Philadelphia in 1859, the *Seaboard* was acquired by Confederate military authorities in 1861. Turned over to the Engineer Corps for operations on the James River, the vessel was captured by the Federal army below Richmond on April 4, 1865.

USS *Seminole.* A 800-ton screw sloop of war, the *Seminole* shelled Confederate batteries on Sewell's Point before performing blockading duty along the Atlantic and Gulf coasts.

USS *Stevens Battery.* *See* USS *Naugatuck.*

CSS *Teaser* (formerly the *York River*). A tug purchased in 1861 by the State of Virginia and assigned to naval forces on the James River, following the state's secession the *Teaser* became a part of the Confederate navy and acted as a tender to the CSS *Virginia* in the Battle of Hampton Roads on March 8–9, 1862. The *Teaser* is famed as a pioneer aircraft carrier and minelayer, since the ship was used to launch a reconnaissance balloon and to lay torpedoes in the James River. While engaging the USS *Maratanza* at Haxall's on the James on July 4, 1862, the *Teaser* was hit by a Union shell, blowing up the boiler and forced the crew to abandon ship. The vessel was taken into the Federal navy and sold at Washington, D.C., on June 24, 1865.

CSS *Thomas Jefferson* (formerly the steamer *Jamestown*). A barkentine-rigged side-wheel passenger steamer built in 1852 for the New York and Old Dominion Steamship Line, the *Jamestown* was seized in July 1861 by Virginia authorities, armed with two guns, and renamed the *Thomas Jefferson*. The ship was scuttled in May 1862 to block the James River channel before Drewry's Bluff.

CSS *Virginia* (formerly the USS *Merrimack*). Following the famed Battle of the Ironclads (also known as the Battle of Hampton Roads) on March 8–9, 1862, the *Virginia,* with its draft of twenty-three feet, was deemed too deep to navigate up the James River and was scuttled on May 11, 1862, off Craney Island.

USS *Wachusett*. A screw-propeller sloop of war built in 1862, the *Wachusett* was armed with two 4-inch Dahlgren smoothbores, one 20-pounder and two 30-pounder Parrotts, four 32-pounder smoothbores, and a 12-pounder rifled gun.

William Allison. A side-wheel steamer of 304 tons used by the Confederacy as a flag-of-truce boat, the *William Allison* was accidentally sunk by Confederate torpedoes in the James River on February 19, 1865.

Bibliography

Unpublished Documents

Brown, Alexander Crosby. "Virginia Pilots: A New Look." Unpublished manuscript, ca. 1984, for the *Daily Press,* Newport News, Virginia.

Curtis, Elvia Theresa Wood. Untitled manuscript of personal reminiscences by a daughter of George Randolph Wood, undated, Mariners' Museum Library, Newport News, Virginia.

Richardson, Emma Wood. "Notes on the Civil War." Seven typed pages transcribed by Thelma Savage, 1959, Library of Virginia, Richmond.

Maps

Davis, Major George B., Leslie J. Perry, and Joseph W. Kirkley. *Atlas to Accompany the Official Records of the Union and Confederate Armies.* Map 1, plate XVII; maps 1 and 2, plate XVIII; map 1, plate XIX; maps 1, 2 and 3, plate LXXVII; map 2, plate LXXXIX; map 1, plate XCII; maps 1 and 2, plate C. Washington, DC: Government Printing Office, 1891–1895.

Gray, O. W. "Gray's New Map of Hampton, Elizabeth City County, Virginia." Philadelphia: O. W. Gray & Son, 1876.

Johnson, A. J. "Johnson's Map of the Vicinity of Richmond and Peninsular Campaign in Virginia." New York: A. J. Johnson, 1862.

Sanborn Fire Insurance Maps of Hampton, Virginia. Ann Arbor, MI: UMI Microfilm, Virginia Reel 6.

Semple, E. A. "Elizabeth City County, Va." Philadelphia: E. W. Smith & Co., 1888.

Newspapers and Periodicals

Confederate Veteran. Vol. XX, no. 4, April 1912.

Daily Press. Newport News, VA, February 12, 1898, and May 30, 1969.

Home Bulletin. Soldiers Home, Hampton, VA, December 6, 1884–November 21, 1891.

News-Herald. Suffolk, VA, August 2005.

The Virginia Magazine of History and Biography. Vol. XXVIII, no. 3. Richmond, VA: Old Dominion Press, 1920.

Other Sources

Allen, Coleen, and Jackie Burroughs, eds. *Identified Gravesites, Oakland Cemetery, Hampton, Virginia*. Hampton: Oakland Cemetery Association, 1984.

Allmendinger, David F., Jr., ed. *Incidents of My Life: Edmund Ruffin's Autobiographical Essays*. Charlottesville: University Press of Virginia, 1990.

Axelrod, Alan. *The War Between the Spies: A History of Espionage During the American Civil War*. New York: The Atlantic Monthly Press, 1992.

Bearss, Ed. *River of Lost Opportunities: The Civil War on the James River, 1861–1862*. Lynchburg, VA: H.E. Howard, 1995.

Beers, Henry Putney. *The Confederacy: A Guide to the Archives of the Government of the Confederate States of America*. Washington, DC: National Archives, 1986.

Bentley, John B. *Gravestone Inscriptions from the Cemetery of St. John's Episcopal Church, Hampton, Virginia*. Hampton, VA: Published for St. John's Church by the Hugh S. Watson Jr. Genealogical Society of Tidewater Virginia, 1975.

Blackiston, Henry C., ed. *Refugees in Richmond: Civil War Letters of a Virginia Family*. Princeton, NJ: Princeton University Press, 1989.

Boatner, Mark Mayo, III. *The Civil War Dictionary*. Rev. ed. New York: David McKay, 1988.

Brock, R. A. *Virginia and Virginians*. Vol. II. Richmond, VA: H. H. Hardesty, 1888.

Butler, Benjamin F. *Butler's Book: Autobiography and Personal Reminiscences*. Boston: A. M. Thayer & Co., 1892.

Calos, Mary Mitchell, Charlotte Easterling, and Ella Sue Rayburn. *Old Point and Hopewell: The First 370 Years*. Norfolk, VA: The Donning Company, 1983.

Cameron, William E. "The Battle of Hampton Roads as Viewed by an Eye Witness." *Richmond Times*, December 30, 1894. Reprinted in the

Southern Historical Society Papers, Vol. XXXII, Richmond, VA, January–December 1904.

Cavanaugh, Michael A. *6th Virginia Infantry.* Lynchburg, VA: H.E. Howard, 1988.

Chataigne, J. H., compiler. *Chataigne's Directory of Richmond, Va., 1882–83.* N.p., n.d.

——. *Chataigne's Peninsula Directory, 1896–97: General and Business Directory of Newport News, Hampton, Chesapeake City and Old Point.* Centennial edition. Hampton, VA: Port Hampton Press, 1996.

Civil War Naval Chronology, 1861–1865. Washington, DC: U.S. Naval History Division, Office of the Chief of Naval Operations, Navy Department, n.d.

Collins, Darrell L. *46th Virginia Infantry.* Lynchburg, VA: H.E. Howard, 1992.

Copland, Mary Ruffin, ed. *Confederate History of Charles City County, Virginia.* Charles City: Harrison-Harwood Chapter, United Daughters of the Confederacy, n.d.

Coski, John M. *Capital Navy: The Men, Ships, and Operations of the James River Squadron.* Campbell, CA: Savas Woodbury, 1996.

Cresson, William Penn. *James Monroe.* Chapel Hill: University of North Carolina Press, 1946.

Current, Richard N., ed. *Encyclopedia of the Confederacy.* 4 vols. New York: Simon and Schuster, 1993.

Curtis, Richard A. *History of the Famous Battle Between the Iron-Clad* Merrimac, *C. S. N., and the Iron-Clad* Monitor *and the* Cumberland *and* Congress *of the U. S. Navy.* Richmond: Museum of the Confederacy, http://cssvirginia.org/vacsn4/original/cr1907.htm.

Dabney, Virginius. *Richmond: The Story of a City.* Revised edition. Charlottesville: University Press of Virginia, 1990.

——. *Virginia: The New Dominion, A History from 1607 to the Present.* New York: Doubleday, 1971.

Dickinson, Jack L. *16th Virginia Cavalry.* Lynchburg, VA: H.E. Howard, 1989.

Dictionary of American Naval Fighting Ships. Vols. 1–9. Washington, DC: Naval Historical Center, 1959–1991.

Dubbs, Carol Kettenburg. *Defend This Old Town: Williamsburg during the Civil War.* Baton Rouge: Louisiana State University Press, 2002.

Dunaway, Wayland Fuller. *History of the James River and Kanawha Company.* Volume CIV. Studies in History, Economics and Public Law. New York: Columbia University, 1922.

Eicher, John H., and David J. Eicher. *Civil War High Commands.* Stanford, CA: Stanford University Press, 2001.

Elliott, Charles F. *Fox Hill: Its People and Places. A History of Fox Hill, Virginia.* Privately printed by the author, 1976.

Engs, Robert Francis. *Freedom's First Generation: Black Hampton, Virginia, 1861–1890.* Philadelphia: University of Pennsylvania Press, 1979.

Evans, Clement A., ed. *Confederate Military History.* Vol. 3. Dayton, OH: Morningside Bookshop, 1975.

Evans, Sandidge. *Lost Landmarks of Old Hampton, Revolutionary War Port Town.* Hampton, VA: The Woman's Club of Hampton, 1985.

Faust, Patricia L., ed. *Historical Times Illustrated Encyclopedia of the Civil War.* New York: Harper & Row, 1986.

Flanders, Alan B., and Capt. Arthur C. Johnson Jr. *Guardians of the Capes: A History of Pilots and Piloting in Virginia Waters from 1611 to the Present.* Lively, VA: Brandylane Publishers, 1991.

Foster, A. J. *Early James River History in and around Hopewell, Virginia.* Falls Church, VA: EconoPrint, 1963.

Fuller-Seeley, Kathryn, Elizabeth Dementi, and Wayne Dementi. *Celebrate Richmond Theater.* Richmond, VA: Dietz Press, 2002.

Gaines, W. Craig. *Encyclopedia of Civil War Shipwrecks.* Baton Rouge: Louisiana State University Press, 2008.

Gibson, Charles Dana, and E. Kay Gibson. *Assault and Logistics: Union Army Coastal and River Operations, 1861–1866.* Camden, ME: Ensign Press, 1995.

———, comp. *Dictionary of Transports and Combatant Vessels, Steam and Sail, Employed by the Union Army, 1861–1868.* Camden, ME: Ensign Press, 1995.

Green, Bryan Clark, Calder Loth, and William M. S. Rasmussen. *Lost Virginia: Vanished Architecture of the Old Dominion.* Charlottesville, VA: Howell Press, 2001.

Greene, A. Wilson. *Civil War Petersburg: Confederate City in the Crucible of War.* Charlottesville: University of Virginia Press, 2006.

Hagemann, James. *The Heritage of Virginia: The Story of Place Names in the Old Dominion.* Norfolk, VA: The Donning Company, 1986.

Hardee, William Joseph. *Rifle and Light Infantry Tactics; For the Exercise and Manoeuvres of Troops When Acting as Light Infantry or Riflemen.* Reprint of 1855 edition. Westport, CT: Greenwood Press, 1971.

Harwell, Richard Barksdale. *Brief Candle: The Confederate Theatre.* Worcester, MA: American Antiquarian Society, 1971.

——. *The Richmond Stage.* N.p., 1955.

Hawkins, Leighman. "Canaling on the Jeems and Kanawhy." *Tracks: C&O Railway Magazine,* vol. 36, no. 1. Clifton Forge, VA: C&O Historical Society, January 1951.

Heffelfinger, Jacob. *Kecoughtan Old and New or Three Hundred Years of Elizabeth City Parish.* Hampton, VA: Houston Printing and Publishing House, 1910.

Hudgins, Garland C., editor. *Recollections of an Old Dominion Dragoon: The Civil War Experiences of Sgt. Robert S. Hudgins II, Co. B, 3rd Virginia Cavalry.* Orange, VA: Publisher's Press, 1993.

Jensen, Les. *32nd Virginia Infantry.* Lynchburg, VA: H.E. Howard, 1990.

Johnson, Robert Erwin. *Rear Admiral John Rodgers, 1812–1882.* Annapolis, MD: United States Naval Institute, 1967.

Jones, Virgil Carrington. *Eight Hours Before Richmond.* New York: Henry Holt and Co., 1957.

Krick, Robert E. *Staff Officers in Gray: A Biographical Register of the Staff Officers in the Army of Northern Virginia.* Chapel Hill: University of North Carolina Press, 2003.

Kunhardt, Dorothy Meserve, and Philip B. Kunhardt Jr. *Twenty Days: A Narrative in Text and Pictures of the Assassination of Abraham Lincoln.* New York: Harper & Row, 1965.

Macaluso, Gregory J. *Morris, Orange and King William Artillery.* Lynchburg, VA: H.E. Howard, 1991.

Magill, Mary Tucker. *History of Virginia for the Use of Schools.* Lynchburg, VA: J. P. Bell Company, 1890.

Marvel, William, ed. *The* Monitor *Chronicles: One Sailor's Account.* Newport News, VA: The Mariners' Museum, 2000.

McCabe, Gillie Cary. *The Story of an Old Town, Hampton, Virginia*. Richmond, VA: Old Dominion Press, 1929.

"Memories of the Days of 1862." *Richmond Times-Dispatch,* Richmond, VA, November 29, 1908.

Miles, Barry W., comp. *Cemeteries of the City of Hampton, Virginia, Formerly Elizabeth City County.* Edited by James H. Mero and Joseph A. Atkins. Published by Tidewater (Virginia) Genealogical Society. Bowie, MD: Heritage Books Inc., 1999.

Mitchell, Betty L. *Edmund Ruffin: A Biography.* Bloomington: Indiana University Press, 1981.

Moore, Robert H., Jr. *Miscellaneous Disbanded Virginia Light Artillery.* Lynchburg, VA: H.E. Howard, 1997.

Munford, George W., ed. *The Code of Virginia.* 2d ed. Richmond, VA: Ritchie, Dunnavant & Co., 1860.

Musick, Michael P. *6th Virginia Cavalry.* Lynchburg, VA: H.E. Howard, 1990.

Nanzig, Thomas P. *3rd Virginia Cavalry.* Lynchburg, VA: H.E. Howard, 1989.

Noel, John V., Jr., and Edward L. Beach. *Naval Terms Dictionary.* 4th ed. Annapolis, MD: Naval Institute Press, 1978.

Official Records of the Union and Confederate Navies in the War of the Rebellion. Ser. 1, vol. 7. Washington, DC: Government Printing Office, 1898.

Owen, Thomas McAdory, and Marie Bankhead Owen. *History of Alabama and Dictionary of Alabama Biography.* Vols. 3 and 4. Chicago: S. J. Clarke Publishing, 1921.

Pinkerton, Allan. *The Spy of the Rebellion: A True History of the Spy System of the United States Army During the Late Rebellion.* Philadelphia: A. G. Nettleton & Co., 1883.

Quarstein, John V. *The Battle of the Ironclads.* Charleston, SC: Arcadia Publishing, 1999.

———. *The Civil War on the Virginia Peninsula.* Charleston, SC: Arcadia Publishing, 1997.

———. *C.S.S.* Virginia: *Mistress of Hampton Roads.* Lynchburg, VA: H.E. Howard, 2000.

———. *Hampton and Newport News in the Civil War: War Comes to the Peninsula.* Lynchburg, VA: H.E. Howard, 1998.

Riggs, David F. *Embattled Shrine: Jamestown in the Civil War.* Shippensburg, PA: White Mane Publishing, 1997.

Robertson, William Glenn. *Back Door to Richmond: The Bermuda Hundred Campaign, April–June 1864.* Baton Rouge: Louisiana State University Press, 1987.

Rouse, Parke, Jr. *The Good Old Days in Hampton and Newport News.* Richmond, VA: Dietz Press, 1986.

——, ed. *When The Yankees Came: Civil War and Reconstruction on the Virginia Peninsula by George Benjamin West, 1839–1917.* Richmond, VA: Dietz Press, 1977.

Rush, Benjamin. *Medical Inquiries and Observations.* 4 vols. Second American Edition. Philadelphia: J. Conrad and Company, et al., 1805

Salmon, Emily, and Edward D. C. Campbell Jr., eds. *The Hornbook of Virginia History: A Ready-Reference Guide to the Old Dominion's People, Places, and Past.* 4th ed. Richmond: Library of Virginia, 1994.

Selden, Jefferson Sinclair, Jr., comp. *The Sinclair Family of Virginia: Descendants of Henry Sinclair.* N.p., 1964.

Starkey, Marion L. *The First Plantation: A History of Hampton and Elizabeth City County, Virginia, 1607–1887.* Hampton, VA: Houston Printing and Publishing House, 1936.

Stensvaag, James T., ed. *Hampton: From the Sea to the Stars, 1610–1985.* Norfolk, VA: The Donning Co., 1985.

Still, William N., Jr. *Confederate Shipbuilding.* Athens, GA: University of Georgia Press, 1969.

Totty, Dale. *Maritime Richmond.* Charleston, SC: Arcadia Publishing, 2004.

Trask, Benjamin H. *16th Virginia Infantry.* Lynchburg, VA: H.E. Howard, 1986.

——. *61st Virginia Infantry.* Lynchburg, VA: H.E. Howard, 1988.

True, Ransom B. *Up and Down the James: An Historical and Contemporary Guide to Places and Life along the James River from Richmond to Hampton Roads.* Research Bulletin 3. Richmond, VA: Association for the Preservation of Virginia Antiquities, 1984.

Tyler, D. Gardiner. *A History and Pictorial Review of Charles City County, Virginia.* N.p.: Expert Graphics, 1990.

Tyler, Lyon G. *Men of Mark in Virginia.* Vol. 3. Washington, DC: Men of Mark Publishing, 1907.

U.S. Department of Commerce, Bureau of the Census. Virginia Census Records for the years 1850, 1860, 1870, 1880, and 1900.

U.S. Department of the Interior, National Park Service. "City Point: Petersburg National Battlefield." Undated historical guide folder.

Wallace, Lee A., Jr. *The Richmond Howitzers.* Lynchburg, VA: H.E. Howard, 1993.

The War of the Rebellion: A Compilation of the Official Records of the Union and Confederate Armies. Ser. 1, vol. 11. Washington, DC: Government Printing Office, 1884.

Weinert, Richard P., Jr., and Col. Robert Arthur. *Defender of the Chesapeake: The Story of Fort Monroe.* 3rd ed. Shippensburg, PA: White Mane Publishing, 1989.

Wharton, H. M. *War Songs and Poems of The Southern Confederacy, 1861–1865.* Reprint of 1904 edition. Edison, NJ: Castle Books, 2000.

Writers' Program of the Works Progress Administration in the State of Virginia. *Virginia: A Guide to the Old Dominion.* Reprint of 1940 edition. Richmond: Virginia State Library and Archives, 1992.

Index

Italicized page numbers refer to illustrations.